TRAINING FOR COMMUNICATION

TRAINING FOR COMMUNICATION

JOHN ADAIR

Gower

© John Adair, 1973

First published in Great Britain in 1973 by
Macdonald and Company (Publishers) Limited

Reprinted 1978, 1979 by Gower Press, Teakfield Limited
Reprinted 1981, 1984 by Gower Publishing Company Limited,
Croft Road, Aldershot, Hants, GU11 3HR, England

British Library Cataloguing in Publication Data

Adair, John
    Training for communication.
    1. Communication in management
    I. Title
    658.4'5   HF5718

ISBN 0 566 02112 9

Printed in Great Britain by
Biddles Ltd, Guildford, Surrey

CONTENTS

ACKNOWLEDGEMENTS

Here I acknowledge with gratitude the aid of the following persons who have kindly read and helpfully commented on this book when it was still in typescript: Peter Bracher, David Charles-Edwards, Professor Derek Newman, John Benjamin, Lady Margaret Brown and John Garnett C.B.E. Also I should add my warmest thanks to Miss Penelope Hoare, the editor who has guided this book, as well as its two predecessors, to completion with her customary grace and efficiency. May I associate with her the whole staff of Macdonald, with whom I have had such a happy relationship. In addition I much appreciate the encouraging and constructive suggestions I have received from the managers who have already taken part in the experimental Whitbread's courses. All advances in training come from such partnerships, and I am conscious how much I owe to all those who have been involved in planning, leading and evaluating the courses. Nor will the reader be in any doubt that I have gained much from my friends and colleagues in The Industrial Society, beyond those mentioned by name above, although I fear that I have not done justice to their great contribution in this field.

INTRODUCTION

Many social changes during recent years have highlighted the need for better communication. The increased complexity and pace of life, the rising standards of education, ever larger organizations, rising personal expectations in the work situation and the impact of television: these are some of the factors creating the greater need for communication. But meeting that need is not an easy matter. Although communication among humans is potentially so much more rich, varied and important than that of our nearest relatives in the animal world, yet it is more prone to error, breakdown and disaster. Those who climb high must risk the worst accidents. Only by understanding and practising good communication can we hope to win the rewards and avoid the penalties of the ascent of man.

In the last decade a number of books with 'Communication' in their titles have appeared. On inspection they often prove to be textbooks in the narrower sense, limiting themselves to the techniques of the subject – how to set out a business letter, when to use a colon, and so on. This present book is not a substitute for these manuals, be they written for students or businessmen; it is designed to complement them. Its main aim is *to describe and explore the art of communication in such a way that you may feel inspired to set about a practical programme for improving your own communicating.* These 'follow-up' steps may well include recourse to the more technical or specialized literature, should you judge yourself to be in need of it. At the back I have included some notes, references and guides for that purpose.

Each chapter has a concrete objective in relation to the central theme above. In the first chapter, for example, the nature of human communication (in contrast to that of animals) and some models of the communication process are respectively considered. The Communication Star model in Chapter Two is introduced as a visual means of showing the essential relatedness of the elements in communication. The case history which follows – 'The Fatal Order' – gives you the reader an opportunity for analysing a really bad example of communication in the light of the opening two chapters. 'Histories make men wise' wrote Lord Bacon optimistically. Certainly wise men do learn from the mistakes of others.

The worlds of industrial, commercial and professional work may seem far removed from the Crimea in 1854, and so they are in many ways. But the problems of communication in large organizations are still very much with us. The first step towards their solution lies in understanding what should be the *aims* and *content* of communication in human enterprises, and this is the subject of Chapter Three. Then in Chapter Four the *methods* of communication appropriate to the corporate and individual needs in organizations are outlined.

Clarity over content and methods, however, is only half the battle. The skills of the persons involved are also vitally important. The four chapters that follow concentrate on two more elements in the Communication Star: the *sender* and *receiver*. Although non-verbal communication continues to play a role alongside language, it is the latter which bears the main traffic of ideas and information. Thus it is our proficiency in oral and written communication, through the complementary skills of Speaking and Listening, Writing and Reading, which enable us to contribute in a direct personal way to the achievement of greater human understanding.

A fifth element in all communication is the *situation*, or the particular circumstances in which it takes place. This general word stands for a variety of meanings, ranging from the physical setting to the social or cultural *milieu* of a given organization or community. There is also a sense in which the roles we fill in everyday life create their own recurring situations. The latter are of course always unique, but also they share some aspects in common which makes it possible to discuss them in general terms, at least to some extent. Two such common situations in working life – Meetings and Interviews – form the subjects of Chapters Nine and Ten. Each of these situations could have a whole book written on it, and so I have concentrated only on what in my judgement is the most difficult communication task in them: respectively, the role of leadership in meetings and the giving or receiving of praise and criticism in interviews.

The last two chapters turn to the tasks of developing the vision and practice of people in the art of communication. Another increasingly common situation in working life – the training course – provides an opportunity for learning about communication. Chapter Eleven seeks to demonstrate how the logical sequence of thought suggested by the Communication Star can be put to work in order to produce a brief but effective programme tailored to the needs of a given organization.

Not all of us, however, can attend courses. Chapter Twelve sets out an alternative (or complementary) strategy: an action programme in which you can set your own objectives for improving communication over the next three-month period. As a help to this target-setting, there are ten guide-lines for action, which are worth considering. Obviously not all of these can be tackled at once, but they should form a quarry for ideas on what to do next. Knowing that a challenge to action awaits you in Chapter Twelve you may find it useful to have a pencil and paper at hand as you read the earlier chapters so that you can write down any action possibilities which occur to you.

Although I have written this book primarily with the manager (in the wider senses of the word) in mind, communication happens whenever two or more human beings are together. Husbands, wives, parents, children, lovers, friends, acquaintances and strangers: we all communicate one with another. By itself good communication cannot cure all our problems, corporate or personal, for the solutions of those depend upon other factors as well. But an awareness and understanding of the nature and practice of good communication can help to identify those problems, as well as the opportunities which they wantonly disguise. Moreover, beyond its limitless practical uses, the art of communication can add so much value and enjoyment to our common act of living in all its aspects.

CHAPTER ONE

THE NATURE OF COMMUNICATION

The peoples of the world are islands shouting at
each other across a sea of misunderstanding

GEORGE ELIOT

These words remind us that lack of communication is endemic in our human condition. Loud shouting and even violence is a symptom of the ailment, not a remedy. Without communication we remain isolated, stranded on our islands, divided rather than united. To diagnose the nature of communication is as important for us now (as individuals, groups and nations) as the discovery of the secrets of the atom for our fathers. We have to discern the forces which create human unity – not those which split matter with a crash – invisible forces which can conquer the 'sea of misunderstanding' and bind our hearts together. The technical problems of long-range communication have been solved; the more central and elusive nature of good communication in human relations remains to be charted.

But what does this long, formidable word mean? Some verbal archaeology may help. Using the *Shorter Oxford English Dictionary* we can unravel the meanings that the word 'communication' has acquired down the centuries. First, it comes from the same Latin root as 'common', namely the word *communis*, whose own roots are shrouded in mystery. The first part of it presents no difficulties, for 'com' is known to be an English version of *cum* (with). The second part, *munis*, descends either from *moinis* (bound), or from the early Latin *oinos* (one). Dr Johnson defined the first and major family of meanings of the word 'common' thus: 'belonging equally to more than one'.

Our medieval forefathers used 'common' as a verb much as we use 'communicate' nowadays. Until the beginning of the first Queen Elizabeth's reign in the mid-sixteenth century an Englishman might have spoken of 'commoning' with his friends about his work instead of communicating with them. He might equally have meant, however, by 'commoning' that he was eating with them at a common table in the great hall of some manor house or college, pasturing his pigs on the common land, or partaking in the Holy Communion or mass at the parish church. Behind all these uses is the central idea of *sharing*: something is available for all to share in it. Thus it is general and not private, a joint rather than an individual possession, one which is accessible freely to others.

'To communicate', which entered the language about the time that Henry VIII was having problems with his six wives, took over the senses of giving to another as a partaker, and making available something for a general sharing. 'Communication' came to mean the action of imparting, conveying or exchanging, or, concretely, that which is communicated, such as a letter or its contents. Although the Christian religion, always conservative when it comes to language, has retained 'communicate' and 'communion' for the sharing of the sacramental elements of the Eucharist, the words are now rarely used in regard to material things. Almost exclusively communication now refers to the giving, receiving or sharing of ideas, knowledge, feelings – the contents of the mind, heart and spirit of man – by such means as speech, writing or signs.

Quite early in its history, however, communication took on the extra job of denoting the access or means of access between two or more persons or places. By 1684, for example, it was used to describe an alley or passage; much earlier, in the English Civil War, the trenches and ramparts connecting the star-shaped forts around London were called the 'lines of communication'. When an army campaigned in the field, however, its lines of communication were the routes or means which linked it with base and with other allied armies: the roads, rivers or canals which made possible the essential communication or sharing of intentions, information and results. The term 'communications' now covers all the latter-day additions to the primitive trench or passage way: telegraph, telephone, radio, television. The distinguishing feature of these modern inventions is that they enable rapid communication between persons widely separated ('tele-' comes from a Greek word meaning 'far off').

Thus we may fruitfully distinguish three strands in the pedigree of communication, each of which still colours our use of the word. First, it means that which is shared, the 'commons', be they bread, land, ideas or life itself. More specifically, as the English language flowered, communication stood for the action of sharing in the mental or non-material realm, especially in and through the use of words. Lastly, anything which links two or more persons or places has come to be called a communication. In other words, communication has come to include the means used as well as the primary activity itself.

The Roots of Communication

We can perhaps learn more about the distinctive nature of communication in humans if we glance first at the world of animals, birds and fish. Wherever we look in the animal kingdom we find that communication through the senses is less liable to error than in man, but it is much more limited. Man, with his infinitely richer potential, is capable of attaining a communion with his fellows and his universe which is beyond the reach of even the most developed animal. Yet his communications are much more likely to go awry than those of his evolutionary cousins and his more distant relatives in the family of the living.

In her study of chimpanzees, entitled *In the Shadow of Man*, the zoologist Jane van Lawick-Goodall emphasized that speech sets humans far ahead of their nearest primate cousins, but that we retain many of the primitive methods of communication observable in the chimp.

In fact, if we survey the whole range of the postural and gestural communication signals of chimpanzees and humans, we find striking similarities in many instances. It would appear then, that either man and chimp have evolved gestures and postures along a most remarkable parallel, or that we share with the chimpanzees, an ancestor in the dim and very distant past; an ancestor, moreover, who communicated with his kind by means of kissing and embracing, touching and patting and holding hands.

One of the major differences between man and his closest living relative is, of course, that the chimpanzee has not developed the power of speech. Even the most intensive efforts to teach young chimps to talk have met with virtually no success. Verbal language does indeed represent a truly gigantic stride forward in man's evolution.

All the same, when humans come to an exchange of emotional feelings, most people fall back on the old chimpanzee-type of gestural communication – the cheering pat, the embrace of exuberance, the clasp of hands. And when, on these occasions, we use words too, we often use them in rather the same way as a chimpanzee utters his calls – on an emotional level.

It is only through a real understanding of the ways in which chimpanzees and men show similarities in behaviour that we can reflect, with meaning, on the ways in which men and chimpanzees 'differ'. And only then can we really begin to appreciate, in a biological and spiritual manner, the full extent of man's uniqueness.[1]

A chimpanzee or an otter, however, are less likely to misinterpret one of their kind touching or clasping them in the presence of some anxiety-producing threat than, say, a pretty girl whose hand is suddenly held by her neighbour in a descending airliner. The repertoire of signs, gestures and postures is limited, and all the animals seem to know the code. The nature of man greatly confuses the issue. Not only is his speech an infinitely varied weaving and interweaving of forty different sounds, but the resulting words are capable of many different interpretations. Hence a man can convey or communicate much more widely and more deeply than a chimp can with his fellows, but at the risk of being more misunderstood and more isolated than any in the animal kingdom.

The limitations of animals can be further illustrated by considering the conditions which are necessary if they are to learn even the most elementary lessons. In 1959 Sir James Gray FRS summarized many experiments with animals by advancing five principles:

1. The response expected must not be unduly complex; the animal must be able to reach the food or escape the danger by making reasonably simple movements. In other words the problem must not be too difficult.
2. The lesson must be presented to the animal under conditions which ensure freedom from extraneous disturbance. An animal will not learn if its attention is constantly diverted by other changes in the environment.
3. The problem must be presented on an adequate number of occasions; the more frequent the lesson the fewer the mistakes.
4. There must be an 'incentive' to learn – a reward for success or a punishment for failure. Further, the reward must be related to the needs of the animal.
5. Finally, the experimenter must possess adequate skill and patience. Ability to learn depends to a very large extent on the personality and enthusiasm of the teacher.[2]

Humans far transcend animals, but we can trace some of the roots of human communication in such experiments: namely that factors in the content, situation, method, subject and teacher must all come into play. Certainly simplicity and repetition retain their value in all instruction or learning. But there is another legacy from our evolutionary past. Despite our development of language we retain *non-verbal communication* as an important auxiliary system.

Non-Verbal Communication

For some years Mr Michael Argyle, of the Institute of Experimental Psychology at Oxford University,[3] has been investigating the 'undercover language' of facial expressions, eye-contact and tone of voice. For example, films of conversations show that the talker tends to look away while actually speaking, but to glance up at the end of sentences for some reaction from the listener, which usually takes the form of a nod or murmur of assent. He gives the listener a longer gaze when he has finished what he has to say.

There are at least eight other factors involved in the non-verbal repertoire: physical touch, appearance (clothes, hair, etc.), posture, proximity, facial expression, hand and foot movements, head position and tone of voice. For the most part these are natural or unconscious expressions of our feelings, synchronized with what we are saying or doing consciously.

It follows that one can only change non-verbal behaviour by changing the inner nature which it is expressing. Courses or conferences which aim to teach you what Shakespeare called 'the craft of smiles' are to be regarded with suspicion, although Mr Argyle's work with mental patients suggests that one can help those whose synchronization has gone sadly awry.

Courses for normal people in such matters as eye-contact or gesture, could only induce self-consciousness, which works against natural communication. What is important, however, is the *awareness* that other people are receiving all our non-verbal behaviour, and perhaps finding it expressive of certain unseen inner states or attitudes which may or may not be there. One can legitimately strive to avoid sending out the wrong signs or signals through the variety of non-verbal channels. Fortunately we now have language, which can in part rectify our mistakes. But it is the original integrated combination of words and signs which make up the rich texture of human communication. We must now turn to our unique capacity for communicating through language – the prime means of human intercourse.

Communication as Dialogue

Most people seem to regard spoken communication as getting a message across to another person: 'You tell him what you want him to know.' This concept implies a one-way traffic from one person to another, with all the emphasis being on transferring a message from one mind to another. Of course we all do this constantly, for example when we tell a taxi driver our destination. But there are some people who have a semi-conscious theory that this is what communication is all about. If this theory is combined with an ingrained self-centredness, it can produce the phenomenon of the bore: one who insists on monopolizing the conversation to transmit *his* messages, regardless of the needs or interests of his hearers. Bores are an ancient social scourge. In 1611 the dictionarist Randle Cotgrave could define a 'monologue' as 'one that loves to heare himselfe talke.'

In its strict sense monologue means speaking alone. It became a theatrical term for a scene in which a person of the drama speaks alone, and hence to its modern use of a dramatic composition for a single performer. By the mid-nineteenth century it had extended its meaning to cover all talk or discourse which resembled a soliloquy. In theoretical terms monologue implies today an emphasis upon one-way communication, with a corresponding lack of awareness of the importance of dialogue: of listening as well as speaking, of sharing instead of giving.

'Dialogue', which means literally a conversation between two or more persons, comes from the same Greek verb as 'dialectic' — the art of critical examination into the truth of an opinion. In early English, dialectic was simply a synonym for 'logic' as applied to formal rhetorical reasoning; in later philosophy, however, it began to take on shades of meaning which still colour its use in our time. Hegel (1770–1831) applied the word dialectic to the process of thought by which the mutually contradictory principles of science, when employed on objects beyond the limits of sensory experience (e.g. the soul, the world, God), are seen to merge themselves in a higher truth which comprehends them. Thus we may speak of a dialectic method of critically inquiring into truth, one in which a dialogue between apparently conflicting views is more appropriate than a reflective soliloquy by a lone thinker.

It is important to distinguish between monologue and dialogue as *methods* of communication on the one hand, and as *theories* or *assumptions* about communication on the other. There is room for a diversity of methods, but we need to constantly rediscover the essential unity of the nature of communication as a shared or common activity. If you close your eyes now and stop reading you will effectively end the communication between us. You are involved in it as much as I am: we are partners in crime. Somehow I have to lead you to make up the deficiencies in my book with your thoughts. If one of us fails, then the communication falls to the ground. The real fallacy of the monologist philosophy is that it ignores your and my contribution to the communication process. Monologue sees us as a passive audience; dialogue knows that the other person holds some of the cards that will give to or withold meaning from both of us. Thus one of the outward signs of a person who is truly convinced that communication is dialogue is that he will be as much interested in knowing about the person with whom he wishes to communicate as he is knowing about the subject in question.

Consequently an awareness of the other person or persons as active contributors to the 'commoning', and not as passive receivers, is an unseen *dimension* which can influence any form of communication. Sometimes it is difficult for the learned or wise to believe that their listeners or readers have anything to add except 'amen'. 'The monological argument against the dialogical process is that the ignorant and untutored have nothing to contribute, so that the addition of zero and zero equals zero', writes Dr Reuel L. Howe.

> This kind of comment, which is made by surprisingly intelligent and otherwise perceptive people, and too often by educators, demonstrates how little they know about the processes of learning. Nor does it follow that the dialogical principle forbids the use of the monological method. There is a place for the lecture and for direct presentation of content, but to be most useful they should be in a dialogical context. Furthermore, it is quite possible for a person giving a lecture to give it in such a way that he draws his hearers into active response to his thought, and although they remain verbally silent, the effect is that of dialogue.
>
> As a matter of fact, one should not confuse the different methods of teaching with the dialogical concept of communication. Both the lecturer and the discussion leader can be either monological or dialogical, even though they are using different methods. The person who believes that communication, and therefore education, is dialogical in nature, will use every tool in the accomplishment of his purpose. When the question needs to be raised, he may use the discussion method or perhaps some visual aid. When an answer is indicated, he may give a lecture or use some transmissive resource. But his orientation to his task is based on his belief that his accomplishments as a leader are dependent partly upon what his pupil brings to learning, and that for education to take place their relationship must be mutual.[4]

Dialogue is nothing more than good conversation: two persons

19

face-to-face, talking and listening to each other, perhaps using gestures and signs as well. Seven characteristics of such conversations have been suggested:

It is face-to-face.
It is a two-way process.
It is informal.
It is sincere and open.
It is adapted to the situation in which it occurs.
It constitutes a means to an end.
It is desired and enjoyable.

Communication tends to be effective in situations which resemble the direct face-to-face conversation, and less effective the less similar they are. If one person cannot see the other, for example, something is already lost from the equation. Dialogue stands close to the heart of communication.

FEEDBACK

A major contribution to our understanding of communication has come from the introduction of the concept of *feedback*. Norman Wierner coined this term in 1946 in an influential book entitled *Cybernetics: or Control and Communication in the Animal and the Machine*. In it he compared communication to a system which loops back on itself: the parts are linked together in a cycle of activity, like a child's electrical train set. Information does not just pass downwards or outwards: it curves backwards like a boomerang and affects the communicator. This phenomenon of bouncing back, the return of information through the system, Wierner called *feedback*.

This model, and instrumental metaphor from the electrical and electronics fields, emphasized the *two-way* or *dialogue* character of communication. According to this picture, communication was a process in which the sender received feedback from the hearer which might lead him to modify his approach. In diagrammatical terms the nearest representation to the model was a circle, and various forms of the circular model (ovals, rectangles with rounded corners) became popular in the 1950s. There are many versions of it, but the essential idea is the same. This example of the feedback process comes from J.W. Humble's book *Improving Management Performance* (1969)[5]. (p.21.)

It has been hoped that the circular model would portray communication as flexible, dynamic and democratic, as indeed to some extent it does. Moreover the electronics background to the Systems Model provided some good metaphors for some of the failings of communi-

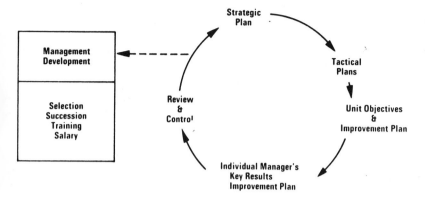

cation in personal and organizational life. For example, William G. Scott could give this thought-provoking list of common faults or communication problems in organizations:

1. *Timing*, i.e. coordinating messages in such a way that they are received either simultaneously or sequentially by different receivers.
2. *Overload*, i.e. reception of messages in such quantity that the receiver is overwhelmed and unable to respond intelligently.
3. *Short-circuiting*, i.e. the omission of one or more persons in a vertical or horizontal communication chain.
4. *Distortion*, i.e. differences in meaning of messages as perceived by senders and by receivers, due primarily to different job or positional orientations.
5. *Filtering*, i.e. conscious manipulation of 'facts' to colour events in a way favourable to the sender (especially upward communication).[6]

The circular or systemic model, however, does have certain drawbacks. Circles and systems can imply a concentration on social maintenance. The cyclic model also evokes some prevalent and largely unexamined assumptions about the nature of society and meaning of history. The circle image, of things returning to their starting points like the change of the seasons, has never entirely satisfied Western civilization. For better or worse we want to push onwards along a line into the unknown. 'Better fifty years of Europe than a cycle of Cathay' as Tennyson declared in the last century.

More recently attempts have been made to develop the circular model while retaining the cybernetic dimension of communication as a dynamic process. A cork-screw? A mattress-spring? One ingenious suggestion, along these lines, comes from Frank E.X. Dance, the editor of a symposium entitled *Human Communication Theory* (1967). Having noted the limitations of the circular model ('a word once uttered cannot be recalled'), he suggested that the recently discovered structure of the DNA molecule might provide the clue, namely the double helix – or a spiral that looks like a coiled ladder. Professor Dance regarded the helix and spiral as essentially the same, however, and offered this model for communication:

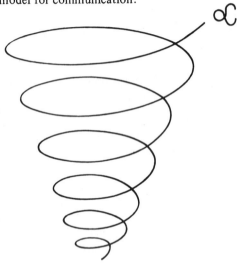

'The helix combines the desirable features of the straight line and of the circle while avoiding the weakness of either', wrote Professor Dance:

> In addition, the helix presents a rather fascinating variety of possibilities for representing pathologies of communication. If you take a helically coiled spring, such as the child's toy that tumbles down staircases by coiling in upon itself and pull it full out in the vertical position, you can call to your imagination an entirely different kind of communication than that represented by compressing the spring as closely as possible upon itself. If you extend the spring halfway and then compress just one side of the helix, you can envision a communicative process open in one dimension but closed in another. At any and all times, the helix gives geometrical testimony to the concept that communication, while moving forward is at the same moment coming back upon itself and being

affected by the curve from which it emerges. Yet, even though slowly, the helix can gradually free itself from its lower-level distortions. The communicative process, like the helix, is constantly moving forward, and yet is always to some degree dependent on the past, which informs the present and the future. The helical communication model offers a flexible and useful geometrical image for considering the communication process.[7]

If nothing else, Professor Dance's article illustrates how the contemporary student of communication often turns to the natural sciences for his metaphors or models.

Conclusion

The word communication embraces a wide range of meanings centring on the concept of *sharing*. It includes the means as well as the ends of human intercourse. The major steps forward in our understanding of its nature in the past fifty years can be summarized by the sequence of the following sentences, which are the milestones, so to speak, marking the main road of research and inquiry:

Communication is one person giving a message to another.
Communication is essentially a dialogue: it takes two to communicate.
Feedback, or the response of the listener modifying the behaviour of the sender, is especially important.
Non-verbal communication, which can be studied in animals, continues as a dimension or aspect in human society.

CHAPTER TWO

THE COMMUNICATION STAR

Communicating is the art of being understood.
PETER USTINOV

In the first chapter the importance of the receiver as a positive contributor to the achievement of understanding has been emphasized. But there are other elements involved in the 'commoning' of any matter. In this chapter these will be identified and discussed with the help of the model I have called the 'Communication Star'. The point of this model is that it illustrates visually the essential inter-relatedness of the elements or aspects of communication. But it is far from perfect, and you may be prompted to build your own model by its very inadequacies. In other words, its purpose is to keep you thinking, not to bring our discussion to a halt.

There seem to be six key aspects to communication. First, there is the *communicator* – the person who has something to share. Secondly, there is the intention or *aim* which lies behind the communication. Thirdly, there is the other person or persons, the receivers or *communicants*. The *content* or matter of the communication – whatever it may be – forms the fourth main ingredient. Fifthly, the means or *methods* of the communication constitutes an independent element in its own right. Lastly, the context or *situation* in which it all takes place influences the nature and outcome of all communication.

These six aspects or elements stand in a complex relationship of inter-action upon each other, as we shall see presently when we look at the salient factors to be considered under each heading. We tend to regard them from the viewpoint of the communicator. One way of developing understanding of communication is to look at it from other viewpoints. We could imagine the elements as billiard balls, which can be sized up from different angles. Or possibly as the outer points and centre of a star, joined and defined by lines of relationship thus:

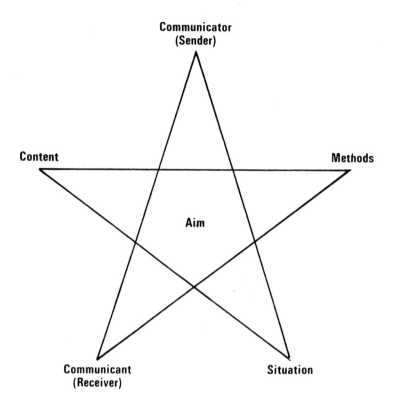

It is tempting to put arrows on the linking lines and to make it into a dynamic process. But this would be an oversimplification, a return to the one-way traffic idea. The influences between the points are tidal: they ebb and flow in both directions. Thus the diagram is alive in that it moves, contracts and propels itself forward in time and space, like an amoeba. Unlike that amorphous creature, however, there are the six 'elements' to which the mind can constantly return.

What then are the relationships between these variables? Obviously there is some sort of relationship between sender and receiver, but quite what character it has will vary: in fact it will always be unique. There is also (or ought to be) a relationship between content and methods, but again the nature of the link between them will vary very widely from instance to instance. In fact a major proposition might be that all six factors have a complex interconnection with each other, and that in studying any one instance of communication we are looking at a particular pattern of relationships between them. Then the skein of wild geese change formation and the same flock of birds arranges itself into a new pattern arrowed across the evening sky.

Thus all of them are connected with each other, albeit by a somewhat roundabout route in some cases. We may postulate that the communication is likely to be good when there are strong and positive lines of relationship defining all six constants. This general point can be illustrated and confirmed by examining each of the headings in turn.

THE AIM

Ideally the aim should stand at the centre of the star, shared by the persons concerned and served by the content, methods and situation. If the intention is only in one person's mind and remains obstinately there without moving out into the middle, then the work of communication is unlikely to be successful. The art of communication lies largely in creating a sense of a common aim. Communication is not two people gazing into each other's eyes; it is two or more looking together at a common question, problem or opportunity; in other words, it is a means to an end.

The word 'aim' is to be understood here as standing between purpose and objectives on a scale ranging from the abstract to the concrete. A purpose is a general direction, a broad river fed by (and feeding) its tributary aims and small stream objectives. The latter are usually concrete goals or targets, designed to be achieved in some tangible way and in a short space of time. An aim need not be quite so concrete or short-lived: it unites the sweep of the large purpose with the earthiness of objectives, and hence can well stand for the intentional heart of human communication.

Usually it is possible to define one's aim in terms of the results which should follow from the communication. These may fall into broad areas, such as change, commitment, action, or understanding. It is then necessary, if possible, to break them down to more specific objectives by asking 'What change?', 'Commitment to what?' or 'Understanding what in particular?'

Besides working downwards from the key words denoting aim or intention, it is also necessary occasionally to work upwards. The ultimate purpose of all human communication may be threefold: to further the common enterprise of humanity; to create and express unity; and to build up the personal lives of individuals. The overlap between these three areas, ever changing as the centrifugal and centripetal forces press it with tensions, may be what we recognize as true peace, the legitimate end of all good communication.

THE COMMUNICATOR (SENDER)

The efficacy of any communication will depend in part on the quality of the communicator or sender, just as music varies with its performer. Thus he or she is one element in any analysis of communication. We are not only the musicians, we are also the musical instruments. The quality and tone of our instrument is made up partly from such more-or-less fixed attributes as our personality, character, intelligence, experience, age and sex. These attributes which go into the making of an individual person are not inanimate pieces of matter: they are living and pulsating, always transmitting their own signals and always colouring our intentional messages with the distinctive sound of the whole person.

Here we come up against the first major factor in the communicator. Perhaps the majority of our communications, as in the cradle, are involuntary: they are the radio waves transmitting ceaselessly by the heartbeats of our conscious and unconscious or depth minds. We do not need Sigmund Freud to remind us that we communicate much more than we imagine we do. Perhaps because it is so essential for survival and evolutionary progress nature has given us an 'over-plus' of communicatory powers. Just as our breathing is involuntary so is our communication with one another. Indeed if we stopped communicating altogether we should die.

Some textbooks write as if communication resembled archery: you carefully select an arrow, flex your muscles, feel the wind, eye the target and then shoot. But communication is not entirely like shooting arrows; it resembles more a bubbling, singing, sometimes roaring, mountain stream, which flows endlessly and is never silent whether we will or no. The task of the communicator is to harness this surging outward-flowing river within him, so that it turns dynamos and lights up the city or adds to the natural reservoirs of common knowledge. This we can do because we are human and personal, not animals or things.

The differences in our make-up are the result of our genetic inheritance and upbringing on the one hand, and how we have responded to them on the other hand. We could say that each of us has a certain inherited potential as a communicator, which a good education will spotlight and develop. This is especially true where the essentials are concerned: the ability to think and to express thought simply, clearly and vividly in words or pictures.

If we carefully studied a highly effective natural communicator — and perhaps we have all met such a person — we should observe that first he is able to share fully what is in his mind if he wishes to do so. As far as the involuntary (or natural) communication is concerned, what comes across either accurately supports what he is consciously saying or else expresses his personality and character in a not unpleasing harmony, although it may strictly be irrelevant to the present matter. The involuntary communication does not conflict with what is seen or heard: there is no jarring dissonance.

Thus the natural communicator is highly adept at using the dams and turbines of language as well as non-verbal pictures and signs to convey his meaning. But, as the image suggests, he is also capable of holding something back. Paradoxically he is also a master of the art of *not* communicating. Much water may find its way around the dam, but it is filtered and sometimes checked in the light of the communicator's general stance or attitude to life and his particular aim. Like a skilled artist he knows instinctively what lines to leave out of the picture.

Our education and training in realizing our potential as communicators begins as soon as we are born. We are conceived and born into a communication system — the family — which we both complicate and enrich. The fundamental skills, at least to a rudimentary level, we acquire early and retain all through our lives. Thus a potential for communication which is always greater than we ever use, and some form of education and training for developing the complex and all-embracing faculty are our birthrights. We evolve the ability because we need it, but the possession of the ability also strengthens the need, like a perpetual-motion machine. This brings us to another major factor in the communicator: his need to communicate.

The natural need to communicate varies greatly in strength from individual to individual, but it is present in some degree in all of us. It furnishes the shadowy background to the more specific and conscious motives or intentions which lie behind actual communications. Our motive for these, the everyday communications at work or home, are a mixture of a subjective and general need to communicate with the more objective necessities of the situation. Where those objective necessities, emanating from outside ourselves, are weak or non-existent, then we either communicate for the sake of communicating or we remain silent. The natural communicator may naturally prefer the second less popular alternative.

Thus much of what passes for communication is really the verbal or visual expression of the need for communication. Nothing is being said, but we are conveying the message that we can talk, that we are human. The need is a natural one, and we become anxious if we meet someone who consistently betrays no need to communicate at all. But we also have to protect ourselves against those with such a strong need to communicate that they impose themselves upon us. We have to guard ourselves against becoming a 'sounding brass or tinkling cymbal'.

Therefore in our profile of 'man the communicator' we may distinguish between three elements. First, there is the inherited potential, both the species-wide faculties such as the seeds of thinking and speaking, and the individual's birth inheritance which includes particular aptitudes for handling different kinds of ideas and the extent and range of verbal facility. Nobody can make a silk purse out of a sow's ear.

Secondly, the influences of family, society and culture, coupled with the quality of the skill-training of early school days, combine to shape us into persons with a certain level of ability for communication. Doubtless Stradivarius chose the best wood for his violins but so did other violin makers. Yet something went into the making of a 'Stradivarius' which transformed all the potential of wood, gut and varnish into a masterpeice for conveying the violin music of his day. We are all different instruments, each specialized for a purpose, but we should all be capable of playing a simple tune. Beyond that it takes the ear of a master to judge special qualities.

Thirdly, to switch over to the woodwind and brass sections of the orchestra, there is the wind in our lungs and our need to blow it out. We are all communicators in that we need to communicate as we need to expire the breath in our chest. The musician can contain that breath longer than most of us; he is trained to direct it aright, and he can refrain from always blowing his trumpet. He has become a musician first and foremost, and only secondly a trumpet player or flutist.

So we are capable of being communicators, and not just talkers or scribblers. But the cost of becoming so is precisely our ability to discipline our tireless need to communicate; to harness it to truly human and personal ends or let it flow sometimes into the reservoirs and cisterns of silence. We have to manage our need to communicate or be managed by it: there is no compromise.

THE COMMUNICANT (RECEIVER)
We all have an inborn potential to recognize meaning in the messages

which come to us. We are natural communicants. We do not, however, all receive the same messages in the same way. Our receiving apparatus is like a computer in that we bring a store of patterns and ready-made interpretations to the work of listening, watching or reading. This transforms the receiving of communications from a passive to an active and positive occupation. As Thoreau said: 'It takes two to speak truth – one to speak and one to hear.'

The sense of meaning is the raw material which makes us into communicants. This capacity to find or give meaning we take with us wherever we go. For some external stimulus to become a communication we have to pick it up on the constantly scanning radar screen of our consciousness; then it has to blaze a light of meaning on that dark hidden inner screen. It is our capacity to perceive meaning which makes us into *homo sapiens*.

Culture and education shape our sense of meaning into certain ranges of 'meanings' and 'interpretations' which we carry with us in more-or-less ready-made packages. At a low level there are simply classifications: the idea of a 'tree' is in my mind, and it leaps to consciousness if I am asked to name the image of that tall swaying thing just outside my window as I write. At a higher level we are capable of filling in, from our own stocks of accumulated meanings, the various signs, signals and symbols which convey messages or meanings to us on frames of reference as fragile as snowflakes.

'Meaning is in the receiver and not in the symbols', wrote G.C. Heaviside, summarizing much research into communication:

> Perception is concerned with the organization of the stimuli we receive and their subsequent interpretation. The way in which we interpret information depends upon the contents of our mental filing-system, our 'stock of labels' or concepts. We are continually acquiring these throughout life as a result of our upbringing, education, training, experience and opportunities. In turn these shape our attitudes and opinions and give us our point of view.
>
> Perception, therefore, is our point of view, our way of looking at life. Two people can receive a similar signal and yet interpret it differently. The same people can receive a similar signal later in life and yet interpret it differently again. Why is it that top management talk about increasing productivity and cutting costs and the man on the floor interprets this as 'sweated labour' and 'redundancy'?.... Perception is principally learned – and we all go through different learning experiences. If the sender and receiver do not share a

common stock of labels, then communication must go astray.'[1]

Perception comes from a Latin word meaning to lay hold of thoroughly. Up to the late seventeenth century, like communication, it could also describe a partaking in the Eucharist. Eventually, however, it came to be used for taking in, or receiving through the mind or senses, again rather like communication itself. We also use it today to describe the ability to apprehend or grasp what is not present to observation, to see through or to see into the less obvious nature or significance of something or someone. The latter may include an intuitive recognition of value, be it moral, aesthetic or utilitarian.

Thus perception, the faculty of perceiving in all these senses, gives us a good idea of the range of contribution which the communicant may offer. He may simply take and receive what is given, through the faculty of comprehension. Or he may interpret something which is not immediately apparent. Or he may have to penetrate inside an opaque communication with a laser beam of intellect. This is always necessary when the communicator does not know what he is trying to say. He may think he does, but even the offering he has measured and cut may contain flaws and grains beyond his own range of understanding, just as a drug may have side-effects unbeknown to the administering doctor.

Moreover to the alert receiver the stream of involuntary and largely non-verbal communication may suggest much about the hidden contents of the communicator's mind, the broad base of the iceberg whose surface shape is being presented for inspection and purchase. Of course it is precisely in these higher reaches of perception, where the rewards. are greater, that the communicant is more likely to misunderstand, mistake and misread the message so tantalizingly veiled from him.

THE CONTENT

Much writing on communication stresses the importance of the skills of the communicator and the receptivity of the communicants. Granted these essentials, so it is believed, the message cannot fail to pass from one to the other. The latter — the receivers — hold the aces because they are the ones who hall-mark the communication with the stamp of meaning. Meaning is subjective; it is given or bestowed by the recipients.

But it may not be quite as simple as that. We certainly do all possess the faculty of *valuing*, the magnetic force which is inwardly attracted to value and meaning. Yet it only contributes half the sum. We need something which has value in it, as an intrinsic property. Although philosophers will continue to debate whether values can be objective in that sense, and the prevailing fashion is to regard all values as the result of projections of meaning from the individual or the social mind, the subjective theory does not work when it comes to the practical business of communication. In the marketplace of ideas we do tend to judge whether the products up for auction are true or not.

This is a vital point, because it removes the whole subject of communication from the realm of what Francis Bacon called 'cunning' and what we should describe as techniques or even gimmicks. Give me any day a nugget with gold streaks in it than a clear piece of glass. This preference on my part springs not from an academic cult of truth for its own sake. Rather it has been my observation that truth does somehow have its own power to communicate. It is as if what is true, or even contains some grains of truth, is like radio-active dust: it has power to transmit its own signals, regardless of its bearer. If the evidences of truth are not present the message may be accepted for a time, but its mortality is assured.

Thus part of the secret of communication is to find something that is true to say — and then let it speak for itself. The fact that the content, or rather the truth in the content, is speaking will make the communicator himself into a listener and a receiver of his own message. It is possible to dress up material in the clothes of a truth, but the proof lies in the eating of the pudding. Quite where we came by this particular value lining to our depth minds I do not know, but we do have a natural power of responding to the power of truth, and an armoury of weapons — some primitive and some highly sophisticated — for penetrating the surfaces and appearances of the food which is presented to us.

The life of a message therefore lies in the truth of its content. The more true it is, gold that is refined or pure, the longer it will be retained in the minds of at least some of the hearers. The communicator is not one who seeks to convey *his* meaning from his own mind to the minds of his listeners. He is a person who has seen or fore-seen some reality, unearthed some facts, discovered some laws and theories, which have for him the ring of truth. For a variety of reasons he wishes to share his discovery of this self-transmitting piece of truth with others. Whether or not they agree with him will not necessarily determine the truth of the matter. He might stand against the world and be proved right. 'The truth is great and shall prevail', wrote Coventry Patmore, 'when none care whether it prevail or not.'

Meals come in various categories of digestibility, however, and the communicator may justly flavour the facts. Like children we sometimes have to be tempted to eat. The mind tends to grasp, accept and retain the simple, logical, known and concrete more than the complex, confused, unknown and abstract. It likes some appetizer or aperitif. Short attractive meals, presented at intervals with plenty of time for digestion in the depth mind, are preferable to dull food replete with truth presented at one gargantuan feast. But it is the truth in the food that matters ultimately, not how palatable it happens to be. Only truths are digested by the mind; lies or half truths always await eventual excretion.

THE METHODS

The fifth element in communication is the means or methods employed. Mistress of all intercourse is language, followed closely by pictures. These are all marks or signs upon paper or in the shape of noises which we use to convey a concept from one mind to another, to share our apprehension of reality. Within the family of language there is a variety of 'ready-made' constructs to hand, the forms made available by our history: conversations, speeches, essays, books, lectures, presentations and letters. Technology has lengthened their arms in the 'tele-' cluster of inventions, just as printing has vastly extended the range of the written word.

These methods or forms – the earthernware jars which carry the action of our communications – also have a life of their own. They are like beasts of burden – horse, oxen, mules, camels – which are pressed into service yet retain their own strengths and weaknesses. Sometimes, like fractious animals, they attempt 'to put the cart before the horse' and take over. Once, when riding in the Jordanian desert, I found myself on a semi-wild camel, who periodically insisted on bending his swan-like neck to bite me. Methods of communication are like that, always trying to buck you off their backs. The means is always potentially in a state of tension with the end; the form declares war on the content.

Methods or means of communication should not dazzle us by their variety or win us by novelty alone. Like old clothes some of the ancient forms of communication are still the most comfortable, practical and serviceable. We cannot avoid using some method or other, and they usually involve language in either the written or spoken versions. But there is an area of choice here. We may not be able to choose what to say, but we can select from several possible ways of saying it.

The general principles governing the choice of means stem from the other elements in the star-shaped pattern of communication, for lines of relation tie them together. First, the communicator should be skilled in that particular medium: it must be part of his repertoire. Skill in one form or medium does not ensure a uniform quality in others. We all develop natural preferences for the elements in which we feel most able to express what is in our mind. Our own history of success and failure in communication predisposes us towards certain methods in which we have developed competence and confidence. But our range is always too limited: there is endless room for self-improvement.

Secondly, the method selected must serve the content; it must be appropriate to the matter in hand. It should not call attention to itself, but set forth the content in question in a self-less way. The prime quality of any means of communication is that it should be *fitting*. We can get by with adequate method, but the communicant's mind pays an extra bonus to the communication if the form is perfectly adapted or appropriate to the end. Thus we may properly speak of 'the art of communication,' for art largely consists of allowing the content to shine through the medium.

Thirdly, the method must match the receivers. There are methods appropriate to age groups and occupations, educational levels and attainments. The receiver has certain expectations as to the methods which he will employ. Surprises may bring delight, but only if the staple diet is conventional. It is important to know the ways in which the customer likes his meals served to him. The uncommon may be more readily received if it is purveyed in a familiar pattern, be that story, lecture or article.

THE SITUATION

The situation in which the communication takes place also exerts its own distinctive influence. Burning decks, for example, are not the best places for long homilies. On the other hand a university campus almost invites lectures. In other words, some methods are more appropriate than others to the actual time and place where the communication occurs.

Of course we can often predict the situation fairly accurately. Providing the communicator has some imagination, he can see in his mind's eye the situation, just as he may be able to sum up in advance the characteristics of the receiver or audience. But, although he may grasp the general situation fairly well, the factors in the specific

34

location can change either dramatically or subtly, like the weather. Hence the communicator needs to be flexible: he has to be prepared to reset his sails when the wind changes, or even take them down altogether and run before the storm.

The situation has little or no power to render a communication satisfactory, but it has considerable potency for throwing spanners in the works. Motor mowers outside the window, the endless clinking of coffee cups, a noisy air conditioner, an over-enthusiastic heating system, arctic cold: the list of distractors is endless. Not only do these attack attention, which is the giving of our minds to the content before us, but they also interrupt the two-way flow of traffic between communicator and communicants. A good communicant may regard such obtrusions as challenges, as occupational hazards to be overcome. But, being human, he may be irritated, especially if the distractions or difficulties could in principle have been avoided.

The situation, however, can have a positive and benevolent influence, albeit a limited one. Old buildings, for example, may acquire a certain atmosphere, a tone of their own, which blends in with the message. If the communication is about contemporary matters, then a bright new building may re-inforce the up-to-date theme. Would Lincoln's address at Gettysburg have sounded quite the same if it had been delivered in the White House garden? Most of the memorable communications of our history have been given in situations which serve as settings for these rare jewels. To summarize: in effective communication the situation is managed so that all the potentially troublesome factors are eliminated; in the best communication the situation supports and encourages the exchange of minds by its silent witness. The communicator, like a good general, is one who chooses his battlefield, and if that cannot be arranged he knows how to employ suitable tactics to minimize its short-comings and maximize its advantages.

Summary

Some aspects of communication we share with other living creatures, especially our ability to express meaning through non-verbal means. Compared with the animal kingdom our means of communication are far greater, but the obstacles are greater too. Alas few of us ever experience the heights of personal communication, as in a truly great love for example, but we all catch glimpses of our unrealized possibilities. We can make a start towards the promised land by grasping that communication means dialogue and not monologue.

Yet, when we look more closely, there is more involved than just two personal centres sharing a common interest or intention. In all human communication there seem to be six major factors involved: communicator, communicant, aim, content, methods and situation. All can serve or hinder the aim. All communication is a pattern of lines or relationships between these points:

COMMUNICATOR: A communication in the deliberate or conscious sense implies a person or persons who sends a message.

COMMUNICANT: If in the language of grammar the sender is the 'subject' then the receiver is the 'object' to whom the message is directed.

AIM: The intention of the message is the purpose in the sender's mind for sending it; it is the reason why there is any communication taking place.

CONTENT: The substance of the message, its component ideas, facts and less obvious value contents.

METHODS: How the message is conveyed, e.g. by writing, speaking or signs.

SITUATION: The context or environment in which the communication is taking place.

If one of the above is totally absent, *per impossibile,* it stands to reason that there would be no communication. The star-shaped diagram is the result of drawing lines of equal length and spacing or arranging the points in order. That simple exercise demonstrates that, although we have to accept the nature of communication as it is, we can bring order into chaos by grasping the intrinsic factors in each of the six aspects or ingredients and manoeuvring them constantly into the right relation or *proportion* with each other in order to serve the aim. The star suggests order in place of chaos: it represents a vision or ideal where all aspects of communication are completely right, and the issue is a communion of spirit, mind and action. We shall probably never reach this star but we all need it for navigation. The Communication Star may thus serve to remind us to consider always the over-all pattern of communication, never just one aspect in isolation from the others.

We can turn the model from a descriptive chart into a practical (or prescriptive) navigating instrument by prefixing each of the terms with an active imperative or phrase, which gives us a standard to reach for. Then we can summarize the nature of communication thus:

Good communication requires an understanding and skilled *communicator*, presenting a true and necessary *content* to an alert and able *communicant*, using the most appropriate *methods* in a *situation* which is contributing to the meeting of their minds, so that the *aim* is fully achieved.

THE CHARGE OF THE LIGHT BRIGADE:

A Case History of Poor Communication

Theirs not to reason why,
Theirs but to do and die:
Into the valley of Death
Rode the six hundred.

The proverbial schoolboy knows the story of the heroic but useless Charge of the Light Brigade at the Battle of Balaclava: 670 horsemen charged on that fateful afternoon of 25 October 1854; 247 men were killed or wounded and 475 horses slain. The immediate cause of the disaster was the misinterpretation of a written message. But behind that failure, so graphically described in the extract from Cecil Woodham-Smith's book *The Reason Why*, which follows, lay a history of strained relations between those who would have to communicate with each other in action.

You may like to space out on a sheet of paper the six elements of the Communication Star, and note the factors under each heading which contributed to the tragic destruction of the Light Brigade.

Lord Lucan (commander of all the cavalry) and Lord Cardigan (the Light Brigade General) had had thirty years of quarrels behind them. More recently Lord Lucan and Captain Nolan (the messenger) had exchanged hot words before Balaclava. And these weak personal links must be set against the general lack of 'team maintenance' or cohesion between staff officers and line commanders, infantry and cavalry, the English and French allies. Thus this glaring instance of bad message writing and passing was but the tip of an iceberg of poor communication; it was upon this cold rock that the Light Brigade foundered.

To appreciate and learn from this disaster it is necessary for the reader to know the essentials of the situation. The Russians in the Crimean War were attempting to intervene in the siege operations before Sebastopol by cutting the British lines of communication to the seaport of Balaclava. The successful charge of the Heavy Brigade and the stubborn defensive resistance of some infantry regiments checked the Russians, but then Lord Raglan, the Allied Commander, spied the enemy attempting to remove some abandoned guns from some high ground to his right. The country is hilly and divided by valleys. Raglan's command post was on the high ground at the head of the long winding North Valley. The Russians occupied the heights on either side of it, and over a mile away, at its other open end, their cavalry was regrouping behind twelve guns. The Light Brigade stood quite near Raglan but, almost on the floor of the valley, thus:

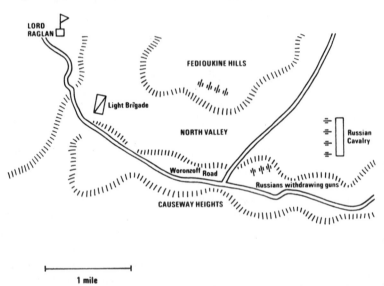

Throughout the story it may be helpful for the reader to bear in mind all the time the simple fact that it was the guns on the *Causeway Heights* that Raglan wished the Light Brigade to secure — not those guarding the Russian cavalry at the end of North Valley. How did Lucan set out towards the wrong objective — and to tragedy? Cecil Woodham-Smith's account is worth studying closely; it is an unforget-table parable of bad communication:

> The charge of the Heavy Brigade ended the second period of the battle. The aspect of the action had been entirely changed by Scarlett's feat. There was no longer any question of the Russians penetrating to Balaclava, they had been pushed away from Balaclava,

even out of the South Valley altogether, and at the moment their position presented difficulties. They held the Causeway Heights and the redoubts, and they had infantry and artillery on the Fedioukine Hills on the other side of the North Valley, but between them the North Valley, 1,000 yards wide, was empty of troops. The troops holding the captured redoubts on the ridge of the Causeway Heights had therefore little support, and Lord Raglan saw that this was the moment to recover the redoubts, the Causeway Heights, and, with the Heights, the Woronzoff Road.

The two divisions of infantry ordered down two hours earlier should now have come into action, but, though the 1st Division under the Duke of Cambridge was present, the 4th Division under Sir George Cathcart lagged behind. He was still in a bad temper, and as he unwillingly left the heights, General Airey had brought him orders to assault and recapture the redoubts – So! he thought, his division, straight from the trenches and exhausted, was to attack, while the Guards were merely marched in support along the valley below. He refused to hurry.

Lord Raglan's anger was evident; indeed, William Howard Russell noticed that Lord Raglan had lost his usual marble calm and seemed fidgety and uneasy, continually turning his glasses this way and that and conferring with General Airey and General Estcourt. He now sent Lord Lucan a third order, of which two versions exist. The copy which Lord Raglan retained in his possession runs: 'Cavalry to advance and take advantage of any opportunity to recover the Heights. They will be supported by infantry, which have been ordered to advance on two fronts.' The order as it reached Lord Lucan and was retained by him is slightly different. The final sentence is divided into two. After the word 'ordered' there is a full stop and 'advance' is written with a capital 'A', so that the final words read 'They will be supported by the infantry which have been ordered. Advance on two fronts.' The change does not affect the issue. Lord Raglan expected Lucan to understand from the order that he was to advance and recapture the redoubts at once without waiting for infantry support, but that infantry had been ordered, and could be expected later.

Lord Lucan read the order in precisely the opposite sense. He was to advance when supported by infantry. Not only did the words of Lord Raglan's order seem to him to have this meaning, but Raglan's treatment of the cavalry throughout the campaign made it highly improbable that he would order an attack by cavalry alone. Again and again, at the Bulganek, at and after the Alma, on October 7th, the cavalry had been restrained, recalled, forbidden to take the offensive, prohibited from engaging the enemy. Only an hour or so ago Lord Raglan had withdrawn the cavalry from their position at the entrance to Balaclava, where they were preparing to engage the Russian cavalry, and placed them in an inactive position under the heights. It never crossed Lucan's mind that he was expected to launch an attack by cavalry with the prospect of being supported at some future time by the infantry. He mounted his division, moved the Light Brigade over to a position across the end of the North Valley, drew up the Heavy Brigade on the slopes of the Woronzoff Road, behind them and on the right, and waited for the infantry, which in his own words 'had not yet arrived'.

Ten minutes, a quarter of an hour, half an hour passed, and the infantry did not appear. Three-quarters of an hour passed, and still Lord Lucan waited. The attack which Lord Raglan wished the cavalry to make appeared to border on recklessness. Redoubt No. 1, on the crown of Canroberts Hill, was inaccessible to horsemen., Nos. 2 and 3 would have to be charged uphill in the face of infantry and artillery. The Heavy Brigade had earlier come within range of the guns in No. 2 and had been forced to retire. However, Lord Raglan, with his power to divine the temper of troops, perceived that the whole Russian Army had been shaken by the triumphant and audacious charge of the Heavy Brigade and that, threatened again by British cavalry, they would retire. Conversations with Russian officers after the war proved Lord Raglan to be right. A feeling of depression had spread through the Russian Army as they saw their great and, as they believed, unconquerable mass of horse-men break and fly before a handful of the Heavy Brigade. For the moment the British possessed a moral ascendancy, but the moment must be swiftly turned to account, and up on the Heights there were murmurs of impatience and indignation as no further action followed the triumph of the Heavy Brigade, and down below Lord Lucan and the cavalry continued to sit motionless in their saddles.

Suddenly along the lines of the Causeway Ridge there was activity. Through glasses teams of artillery horses with lasso tackle could be made out; they were coming up to the redoubts, and a buzz of excitement broke out among the staff. 'By Jove! they're going to take away the guns' — the British naval guns with which the redoubts had been armed.

Captured guns were the proof of victory: Lord Raglan would find it difficult to explain away Russian claims to have inflicted a defeat on him if the Russians had not only taken an important position, but captured guns as well. The removal of the guns must be prevented, and, calling General Airey, Lord Raglan gave him rapid instructions. General Airey scribbled an order in pencil on a piece of paper resting on his sabretache and read it to Lord Raglan, who dictated some additional words.

This was the 'fourth order' issued to Lord Lucan on the day of Balaclava — the order which resulted in the Charge of the Light Brigade — and the original still exists. The paper is of poor quality, thin and creased, the lines are hurriedly written in pencil and the flimsy sheet has a curiously insignificant and shabby appearance. The wording of the order runs: 'Lord Raglan wishes the cavalry to advance rapidly to the front — follow the enemy and try to prevent the enemy carrying away the guns. Troop Horse Artillery may accompany. French cavalry is on your left. Immediate. (Sgd.) Airey.'

Captain Thomas Leslie, a member of the family of Leslie of Glaslough, was the next aide-de-camp for duty, and the order had been placed in his hand when Nolan intervened. The honour of carrying the order he claimed was his, by virtue of his superior rank and consummate horsemanship. The only road now available from the heights to the plain 600 or 700 feet below was little more than a track down the face of a precipice, and speed was of vital importance. Lord Raglan gave way and Nolan, snatching the paper out of Captain Leslie's hand, galloped off. Just as Nolan was about to descend, Lord Raglan called out to him, 'Tell Lord Lucan the cavalry is to attack immediately'. Nolan plunged over the verge of the heights at breakneck speed.

ANY other horseman would have picked his way with care down that rough, precipitous slope, but Nolan spurred his horse, and up on the heights the watchers held their breath as, slithering, scrambling, stumbling, he rushed down to the plain.

So far the day had been a terrible one for Edward Nolan; even its sole glory, the charge of the Heavy Brigade, had been gall and wormwood to his soul. He was a light-cavalryman, believing passionately in the superior efficiency of light over heavy horsemen — 'so unwieldy, so encumbered', he had written — and in this, the first cavalry action of the campaign, the light cavalry had done absolutely nothing. Hour after hour, in an agony of impatience, he had watched the Light Cavalry Brigade standing by, motionless, inglorious and, as onlookers had not scrupled to say, shamefully inactive.

For this he furiously blamed Lord Lucan, as he had furiously blamed Lord Lucan on every other occasion when the cavalry had been kept out of action, 'raging', in William Howard Russell's phrase, against him all over the camp. Irish-Italian, excitable, headstrong, recklessly courageous, Nolan was beside himself with irritation and anger as he swooped like an avenging angel from the heights, bearing the order which would force the man he detested and despised to attack at last.

With a sigh of relief the watchers saw him arrive safely, gallop furiously across the plain and, with his horse trembling, sweating and blown from the wild descent, hand the order to Lord Lucan sitting in the saddle between his two brigades. Lucan opened and read it.

The order appeared to him to be utterly obscure. Lord Raglan and General Airey had forgotten that they were looking down from 600 feet. Not only could they survey the whole action, but the inequalities of the plain disappeared when viewed from above. Lucan from his position could see nothing; inequalities of the ground concealed the activity round the redoubts, no single enemy soldier was in sight; nor had he any picture of the movements of the enemy in his mind's eye, because he had unaccountably neglected to take any steps to acquaint himself with the Russian dispositions. He should, after receiving the third order, have made it his business to make some form of reconnaissance; he should, when he found he could see nothing from his position, have shifted his ground – but he did not.

He read the order 'carefully', with the fussy deliberateness which maddened his staff, while Nolan quivered with impatience at his side. It seemed to Lord Lucan that the order was not only obscure but absurd: artillery was to be attacked by cavalry; infantry support was not mentioned; it was elementary that cavalry charging artillery in such circumstances must be annihilated. In his own account of these fatal moments Lucan says that he 'hesitated and urged the uselessness of such an attack and the dangers attending it'; but Nolan, almost insane with impatience, cut him short and 'in a most authoritative tone' repeated the final message he had been given on the heights: 'Lord Raglan's orders are that the cavalry are to attack immediately.'

For such a tone to be used by an aide-de-camp to a Lieutenant-General was unheard of; moreover, Lord Lucan was perfectly aware that Nolan detested him and habitually abused him. It would have been asking a very great deal of any man to keep his temper in such circumstances, and Lord Lucan's temper was violent. He could see nothing, 'neither enemy nor guns being in sight', he wrote, nor did he in the least understand what the order meant. It was said later that Lord Raglan intended the third and fourth orders to be read together, and that the instruction in the third order to advance and recover the heights made it clear that the guns mentioned in the fourth order must be on those heights. Lord Lucan, however, read the two orders separately. He turned angrily on Nolan, 'Attack, sir? Attack what? What guns, sir?'

The crucial moment had arrived. Nolan threw back his head, and, 'in a most disrespectful and significant manner', flung out his arm and, with a furious gesture, pointed, not to the Causeway Heights and the redoubts with the captured British guns, but to the end of the North Valley, where the Russian cavalry routed by the Heavy Brigade were now established with their guns in front of them. 'There, my lord, is your enemy, there are your guns,' he said, and with those words and that gesture the doom of the Light Brigade was sealed.

What did Nolan mean? It has been maintained that his gesture was merely a taunt, that he had no intention of indicating any direction, and that Lord Lucan, carried away by rage, read a meaning into his out-flung arm which was never there.

The truth will never be known, because a few minutes later Nolan was killed, but his behaviour in that short interval indicates that he did believe the attack was to be down the North Valley and on those guns with which the Russian cavalry routed by the Heavy Brigade had been allowed to retire.

It is not difficult to account for such a mistake. Nolan, the cavalry enthusiast and a cavalry commander of talent, was well aware that a magnificent opportunity had been lost when the Light Brigade failed to pursue after the charge of the Heavies. It was, indeed, the outstanding, the flagrant error of the day, and he must have watched with fury and despair as the routed Russians were suffered to withdraw in safety with the much-desired trophies, their guns. When he received the fourth order he was almost off his head with excitement and impatience, and he misread it. He leapt to the joyful conclusion that at last vengeance was to be taken on those Russians who had been suffered to escape. He had not carried the third order, and read by itself the wording of the fourth was ambiguous. Moreover, Lord Raglan's last words to him, 'Tell Lord Lucan that the cavalry is to attack immediately', were fatally lacking in precision.

And so he plunged down the heights and with a contemptuous gesture, scorning the man who in his opinion was responsible for the wretched mishandling of the cavalry, he pointed down the North Valley. 'There, my lord, is your enemy; there are your guns.'

Lord Lucan felt himself to be in a hideous dilemma. His resentment against Lord Raglan was indescribable; the orders he had received during the battle had been, in his opinion, not only idiotic and ambiguous, but insulting. He had been treated, he wrote later, like a subaltern. He had been peremptorily ordered out of his first position – the excellent position chosen in conjunction with Sir Colin Campbell – consequently after the charge of the Heavies there had been no pursuit. He had received without explanation a vague order to wait for infantry. What infantry? Now came this latest order to take his division and charge to certain death. Throughout the campaign he had had bitter experience of orders from Lord Raglan, and now he foresaw ruin; but he was helpless. The Queen's Regulations laid down that 'all orders sent by aides-de-camp ...are to be obeyed with the same readiness, as if delivered personally by the general officers to whom such aides are attached'. The Duke of Wellington himself had laid this down. Had Lord Lucan refused to execute an order brought by a member of the Headquarters staff and delivered with every assumption of authority he would, in his own words, have had no choice but 'to blow his brains out'.

Nolan's manner had been so obviously insolent that observers thought he would be placed under arrest. Lord Lucan, however, merely shrugged his shoulders and, turning his back on Nolan, trotted off alone, to where Lord Cardigan was sitting in front of the Light Brigade.

Nolan then rode over to his friend Captain Morris, who was sitting in his saddle in front of the 17th Lancers – the same Captain Morris who had urged Lord Cardigan to pursue earlier in the day – and received permission to ride beside him in the charge.

There was now a pause of several minutes, and it is almost impossible to believe that Nolan, sitting beside his close friend and sympathizer, did not disclose the objective of the charge. If Nolan had believed the attack was to be on the Causeway Heights and the redoubts, he must surely have told Captain Morris. Morris, however, who survived the charge though desperately wounded, believed the attack was to be on the guns at the end of the North Valley.

Meanwhile Lord Lucan, almost for the first time, was speaking directly and personally to Lord Cardigan. Had the two men not detested each other so bitterly, had they been able to examine the order together and discuss its meaning, the Light Brigade might have been saved. Alas, thirty years of hatred could not be bridged; each, however, observed perfect military courtesy. Holding the order in his hand, Lord Lucan informed Lord Cardigan of the contents and ordered him to advance down the North Valley with the Light Brigade, while he himself followed in support with the Heavy Brigade.

Lord Cardigan now took an astonishing step. Much as he hated the man before him, rigid as were his ideas of military etiquette, he remonstrated with his superior officer. Bringing down his sword in salute he said, 'Certainly, sir; but allow me to point out to you that the Russians have a battery in the valley on our front, and batteries and riflemen on both sides.'

Lord Lucan once more shrugged his shoulders. 'I know it,' he said; 'but Lord Raglan will have it. We have no choice but to obey.' Lord Cardigan made no further comment, but saluted again. Lord Lucan then instructed him to 'advance very steadily and keep his men well in hand'. Lord Cardigan saluted once more, wheeled his horse and rode over to his second-in-command, Lord George Paget, remarking aloud to himself as he did so, 'Well, here goes the last of the Brudenells'.

CHAPTER THREE

ORGANIZATIONS: CONTENT OF COMMUNICATION

Communication and consultation are essential in all
establishments. They are necessary to promote operational
efficiency and mutual understanding, as well as the individual
employee's sense of satisfaction and involvement in his job.
INDUSTRIAL RELATIONS CODE OF PRACTICE

Sometimes it is tempting to concentrate only on the general need for
communication and the methods available in organizations, neglecting
the central question: 'What should the communication be about?' This
chapter sets out to describe as specifically as possible the topics for
communication. But first it is worth setting the scene by outlining three
factors which have a direct bearing on the content of communication in
organizations: *size, change* and *expectation*.

SIZE
For a variety of reasons, predominantly economic, the prevailing
tendency towards the growth in size of human organizations in almost
every sector of life looks like continuing. Indeed some prophets have
forecast that by the turn of the century we shall all be working for
about 300 universal giants. Be that as it may, the speed towards
corporate bigness has certainly accelerated in the last decade.

But what is a 'large' organization? Would you call a firm of 3,000
employees large, small or medium? As in the case of hills and
mountains, where there is no agreed 'height' which divides them, it is a
matter for individual judgement. Experience suggests that people have
very different internal scales for measuring 'small' and 'large' in human
groupings. To put my own cards on the table, I regard any organization
of more than about 500 people as large, for that number is already
getting beyond the maximum that any one leader can hope to know by
name.

Although it solves many problems by the well-known 'economies of
size', the increased bulk of organizational life creates other ones no less
thorny. Foremost among these is the problem of communication. In
the group or small organization this can be done simply by word of
mouth. In the modern corporation even communication has to be

organized and managed.

Moreover it should not be lightly assumed that the problem of communication afflicts or troubles only the industrial giants, such as General Motors, Fords, Imperial Chemicals or Unilever. The Civil Service (500,000 strong in Britain at present) and the Churches encounter the same difficulty, as do the larger trade unions. For example, *The Times* reported in 1971 the following inquiry:

> Professor Hugh Clegg, of Warwick University, has uncovered some alarming deficiencies in the internal communications of the General and Municipal Workers' Union, third largest union in Britain, with more than 850,000 members. At the G.M.W.U.'s own request, Clegg and a team of graduate students have been finding out whether journals, circulars, educational courses and conferences really keep members in the picture.
>
> In one 3,000-member branch, few knew the name of the union's general secretary – Lord Cooper, for their benefit – and nobody knew where its policy is determined, or that it has a detailed policy on equal pay. The 1,000 members of another branch were a little better informed but only, it seemed, because of the personal efforts of the branch secretary. The G.M.W.U. reports these first findings candidly in its monthly journal, with a warning against complacency and a resolve to improve matters. Other unions will surely be taking note.[1]

In light of the problem of communication so obviously posed by big organizations one would expect to find a mass of research studies on both the needs and the remedies. But there seems to be a strange law that prevents organizations from researching into the really vital aspects of their own working lives – leadership, decision-making and communication. By research I mean objective studies of what actually happened and why it happened that way rather than any other. 'There are very few functional-structural studies of communication, in particular of communication in organizations', concluded A.A. Etzioni in 1961.[2]

Considering the shelves of books with 'Communication' in their titles, the growth of management education and the numbers now engaged in teaching and research on communication, this may seem an odd conclusion. Limited or minor studies touching upon communication certainly exist in the 'tributary' disciplines, such as social psychology, sociology, information (or data) technology and psychology.[3] But these articles and research papers do not look at an organization as a whole; they do not touch upon what really matters.

47

Moreover all too often their own jargon and wooden style makes them into show-pieces of bad communication.

The larger an organization grows the more time and energy it must devote to communication among its parts. Matters concerned with creating or maintaining the spirit and practices of unity must occupy a bigger share of the communication content. The rules, procedures or meetings which ensure co-ordinated effort will inevitably take up more time in the communications within larger organizations than in very small ones. The result is that 'issues like human relations, work on problems of communication and of people understanding one another, which we used to think of as the frills of a business organization, now become absolutely central.'[4]

CHANGE

Communication and consultation are particularly important in times of change. The achievement of change is a joint concern of management and employees and should be carried out in a way which pays regard both to the efficiency of the undertaking and to the interests of employees. Major changes in working arrangements should not be made by management without prior discussion with employees or their representatives.

When changes in management take place, for example, following a merger or take-over, the new managers should make prompt contact with employee representatives and take steps to explain changes in policy affecting employees.

These sentences from the Industrial Relations Code of Practice high-light the importance of good communication in times of change. Change means the intrusion of the new, the unfamiliar or the unknown into the ordered working world; as such it can produce the symptoms of fear, anxiety or insecurity. But the pace and scope of change has accelerated: we all have to live with it and cope with the consequences. Whether or not it is perceived and accepted as progress or rejected as a loss of a way of life will depend as much on the integrity and trust which has been built up in the relationships within the organization, and the presence of good communications, as on the intrinsic merits of the change.

EXPECTATION

In the Second World War more than one commander noted that intelligent soldiers fought much better when they were told what was going to happen. The conditions of modern warfare made close control impossible, and the soldier who knew the plan could use his initiative in carrying it out, even though he was separated from his officers. Moreover it was noted that the simple act of telling men what was the task, and the problems involved in it, had a profound motivational effect. The allied soldier of the Second World War could be driven only with difficulty, but he was easy to lead.

A major difference now is that an ever-growing majority of men and women at work expect not only to be told what they are doing but also why it has to be done that way. In addition they expect to be consulted much more often, if not about the aims at least about the objectives and methods of their daily work. Managers, supervisors, foremen, shop stewards and work people expect their leaders to communicate with them on a regular and thorough basis, just as they recognize the increasing demands made ·on them to communicate with others both within and without the organization. But *any* communication will not suffice. There are certain areas or topics that people want to hear about and discuss.

Topics for Communication
The word 'topic' comes from a Greek term meaning 'place'. The places the Greek writers had in mind were those quarries where orators might find arguments for or against a case. We may use the word to stand for the places where a manager should look for the *contents* of his communications. A brief analysis of organizations will uncover them for us.

In contrast to families, working organizations have a *purpose* to serve, which they break down into the more concerte *aims* and attainable *objectives*.

In social terms to 'organize' means to form into a whole or to create a definite and orderly structure, *for a definite purpose*.

In small teams the characteristics of organization are there in embryo, although it may take the sharp eyes of a social psychologist to discern them. In particular there are some kinds of tasks and allocations of roles which may be single functions or a few functions associated together. In part these roles (made up from functional actions) meet the need to achieve the common *task*; in part they serve to *maintain* and build up the common life of the group; and lastly, they include responses to the recurring needs of individuals, as persons who are both ends in themselves and means towards the common success.

The inter-relations among three areas of need present in working groups can be portrayed by the model of these three over-lapping

49

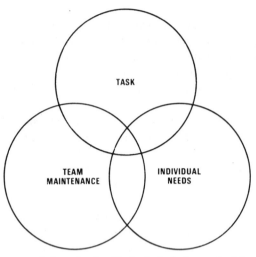

circles. Success or failure in the *Task* circle helps to build up or break down group unity (the *Team Maintenance* need). Also it affects the *Individual* for good or ill, because in a large part his own higher needs (physical, social, esteem, achievement and self-actualization) and values are bound up with the common advance or corporate progress, as well as the quality of the common life. Yet performance rests on the knowledge and skill of individual members, just as the social life of the team rests upon the humour and courage which individuals export into it. The circles are thus inter-acting. But there is also a tension between them, which is important for the understanding of organizations.

The purpose of communication in organizations is usefully defined by the three circles: to achieve the common task, maintain the unity of the whole body and to meet individual needs. Thus the *content* of communication falls into the three (over-lapping) areas:

1. Purpose, aims, objectives, plans and policies.
2. Procedures, rules and normal standards.
3. Conditions of service, performance, progress and prospects.

This conclusion is supported by some research which suggests that these are the subjects people at work want to hear about. A study of two big American firms made by Princeton University in 1949 showed the employees could put to best use these three types of information:

1. Anything which gave them a better insight into their work, and its relation to the work of others in the firm.
2. Anything which gave them a sense of belonging to the firm.
3. Any information which improved their sense of status and importance as individuals in the firm.[5]

50

Priorities for Communication

All managers have to think in terms of priorities, not least when it comes to communications. The three general topics outlined — matters concerned with the common task, team (or organizational) relations and individual needs — have to be constantly scanned in order to select the priorities, which must then be matched by the best-grade methods of communication available. The less important matters can be married off to the less effective communication methods. The manager or management may find it useful to bear in mind three concentric circles of priority to balance the three over-lapping ones:

There will be a mass of material which deserves to be communicated in any organization so it is important at a given time to break it down into:

MUST KNOWS: vital points necessary to achieve the common aim.

SHOULD KNOWS: desirable but not essential.

COULD KNOWS: relatively unimportant.

In industrial organizations there is room for debate on what should fall into the MUST, SHOULD and COULD circles in a specific situation, but generally speaking there is wide agreement on the areas which have to be constantly considered for such priority decisions. Peter Masefield, a former chief executive of British European Airways, has listed — and commented on — these important main categories of key information to the effect that an effective two-way process within a company should deal with this type of information under seven main headings:

First — the policy and objectives of the company, both in broad terms and in their detailed components right down to floor level.

Second — the results and achievements — both financial and general — gained already from the application of the company's policy — together with such modifications of policy as are suggested by experience.

Third — plans and prospects for the future and the basic assumptions on which forward estimates are based.

Fourth — aspects of conditions of service and improvements which are desirable and can be attained.

Fifth — ways and means by which efficiency and productivity can be improved.

Sixth — problems of industrial safety, health and welfare among staff.

Seventh — education — general and specialised.

Under each of these headings we can ask ourselves 'What do the men — and the women — on the shop floor want to know about this aspect of the business'?· And we can also ask ourselves, in addition — 'What do we want to know about their reactions on this subject?' If we are wise, we shall want to know a lot.

In the case of policy in my experience the important thing is 'Why'. The 'why' of the business can range from commercial policy dictating why prices are set at the figures they are, down to such items as why re-equipment is being pressed forward or postponed, why a competitor may have established a particular lead, why advertising is concentrated on certain lines and why profits are ploughed back.

On policy matters above all else, one thing inevitably leads to another. In my experience a full and free discussion can work wonders in improving morale. Such an exchange alone can bring to light facts that lead to a proper understanding of the reasons for given action. Without this background, our decisions may very easily be misunderstood. 'To know all is to support all' — provided management is sound and knows how to express itself.[6]

Integrity and Trust

The ability to communicate implies the equal ability *not* to communicate. There are good reasons as well as bad ones why certain information cannot be briefed or spread throughout an organization. The words 'good' and 'bad' bring us back to the realm of moral judgements. It is important to consider these value dimensions, because they are bound up with the creation and maintenance of trust. If anyone wishes to create good communication in organizations the first essential for consideration (in the Communication Star) is the line of relationship which joins the potential senders and receivers. If that line is strong in trust it will have the necessary reserves to overcome the occasional necessary non-disclosure of information to avoid industrial espionage, for instance. It also will cope with the odd distortion or failure in communication, such as we as fallible humans are prone to commit.

But 'bad' reasons, for example withholding financial information to prevent wage claims, breeds mistrust and impugns the integrity of management. And integrity is the foundation of good communication; techniques are only its servants. Peter Drucker has rightly stressed its importance for the manager or leader of tomorrow in any organization or field:

> 'The more successfully tomorrow's manager does his work, the greater will be the integrity required of him... Indeed the new tasks demand that the manager of tomorrow root every action and decision in the bedrock of principles, that he lead not only through knowledge, competence and skill but through vision, courage, responsibility and integrity.'[7]

Without such leadership our organizations will tend to become impersonal pieces of technology, never achieving full operational effectiveness, let alone mutual understanding and a sense of satisfaction and true involvement for each individual member.

CHAPTER FOUR

ORGANIZATIONS: METHODS OF COMMUNICATION

The first function of the executive is to
develop and maintain a system of communication.
CHESTER BARNARD

Methods are ways of doing things, especially according to regular plans or procedures. A system is a group, set or aggregate of things, natural or artificial, forming a connected or complex whole. Thus any organization has a system of communications, although few managers may be aware of all its ramifications. In order to understand the system in a given organization it is necessary to study it in an objective way. This kind of research is still the exception rather than the rule. Once the profile of the system has been established its strengths can be confirmed and its deficiencies made good. To achieve these improvements, however, it is important to grasp the characteristics and functions of the main methods which form strands in many contemporary organizational systems.

We must first distinguish at this point between the method and the people who are involved in it. A railway network may be judged a good one, even though the diesel engines are slow, the train drivers incompetent and the buffet-car food bad. But the remedies for these ills would not include tearing up the tracks.

The six sections below deal with some of the main methods or systems which many larger organizations have evolved or adopted for handling the increased load of communication that contemporary business and the rising expectations of employees require. Doubtless the reader will be able to add other systems to the list, such as the regular meetings of trade union representatives and management, or annual general meetings.

LINE MANAGEMENT
An obvious line of communication in any organization follows the structure of roles or the hierarchy. The pyramid or tree structure persists, despite the under-mining activities of recent years, simply

54

because large organizations need it for their work. It is true that the degree of participation in policy decisions has increased, and will do so much more in the coming years. But, if nothing more, the implementation of decisions does require a structure of roles with a definition of accountability. Nor should we imagine that a measure of clarity in such matters is antagonistic to human values. Professor D. S. Pugh and his University of Aston colleagues drew this conclusion from their extensive research into organizations:

> Most important of all is the finding that work groups having many standard procedures and rules do not necessarily become dissatisfied and disunited... This supports the view that a reasonable amount of job definition and control by procedures does not lessen readiness to innovate... It is our hope that the publication of our work may help to modify what may be a current over-emphasis on the informal aspects of group behaviour.[1]

Thus, despite its military overtones, the 'chain of command' allows for essential information to flow downwards or upwards in any kind of organization. Moreover this exchange can happen in a series of personal interviews or conversations, which may or may not be formalized. In an age which rather favours group meetings and group discussions it is important to retain the centrality of the one-to-one transmission of instructions, information or ideas. In vital matters there is often a tendency in organizations to revert to fundamentals: to communicate directly to the individual, supporting the spoken word with a letter, memo or report as necessary.

One source of confusion in communication is a lack of understanding of the distinction between *line* and *staff* management. Line authority is exercised by any manager, over his immediate subordinates, and carries the right to direct their work. Staff authority is exercised by a staff manager only over other managers who report to a line manager in common with him, and carries with it the right to advise on how previously agreed policies, plans or procedures should be carried out. Thus the line of authority can be shown by the following diagram, though of course the Staff Manager in it will have a direct line of communication with Line Manager (B) as well.

BRIEFING GROUPS

The personal one-to-one link works well, but in large organizations it needs to be supplemented by briefing groups, just as the modern university has had to introduce seminars to augment the traditional

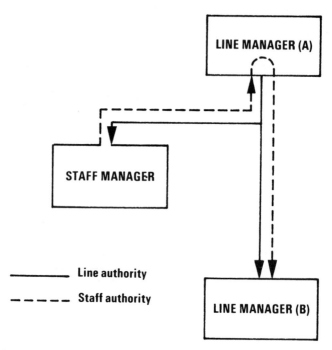

LINE MANAGER (A)

STAFF MANAGER

——————— Line authority

— — — — — Staff authority

LINE MANAGER (B)

one-to-one tutorial system. Briefing groups are the method whereby one communicator passes on orally some instructions or information to a small number of communicants (i.e. not less than two, not more than about 30). It is usually assumed that the communicator will be of a senior status to the group — their leader, manager, supervisor, foreman or chargehand. On the military analogy, such meetings may be *ad hoc* briefings (i.e. before some particular exercise), or they may be formalized so that everyone belongs to a briefing group which meets regularly, not unlike the Army's 'O-Groups' (Order Groups).

Despite its current military use the word 'briefing' comes from the legal world. A brief (from the Latin *breve*) was originally a writing issued by an official or legal authority, such as king or pope. The term survived in the legal profession to mean a summary of facts and points of law, drawn up by a solicitor for a counsel in charge of a case. Thus paradoxically 'to brief' originally meant to put something down on paper. It has always included the notion of brevity, for the ancient documents or letters were comparatively short and terse.

Such is the triumph of oral communication that briefing now stands for a spoken passing on or interpretation of instructions. Whether explicit or not. The Industrial Society has played a leading part in advocating the introduction of such purposeful meetings. In his booklet *The Manager's Responsibility for Communication* (1964, revised 1971), the Society's Director John Garnett proposed the following 'drill':

Each department will organise its systems of face to face communication differently depending on the number of levels and the work arrangements, numbers involved and whether on shifts or days. The system for each department should be written down and made known to all concerned. A typical arrangement would be for a works manager to see his deputies and section heads together; they in their turn would see their plant managers and foremen together, and the foremen would then see the men and act as management's spokesmen. In this way five levels of management would be covered in three 'steps. It might be possible to get the whole management team together at one time but the groups should not be larger than 18. *Understanding* of policies and decisions is only achieved if the group is small enough to allow questions and discussion. Eighteen is normally the maximum.

On many occasions the manager or supervisor will need a written brief to guide him, which may be an abstract of a much larger and complicated administrative document. How often should briefing groups meet? John Garnett suggested these guidelines:

Briefing sessions should ideally only be held when there is something important to communicate. If it is merely left to this, however, there is a danger that in practice sessions will be held only when there is something to tell which is to the employees' disadvantage such as the coming of redundancy or the tightening of an incentive scheme. It is therefore essential to stipulate that a minimum number of meetings are held — at least four a year which, because of holidays, are not necessarily spread equally through the year. Down to the level of supervisor the minimum frequency is eleven times a year.

Lastly, the Industrial Society has emphasized the importance of brevity, proposing thirty minutes as an ideal. Two-thirds of this time should be spent on covering the decisions and policies which affect the work — the nature of his job and the conditions of employment — leaving one-third for questions and points which the working group may want to raise.

The evidence suggests that briefing groups are a most valuable practice. So many organizations have now adopted this method on a regular basis that any example must be a random one. At a conference[2] in June 1971 various speakers discussed this topic. Michael Bewes, Personnel Manager of the Guardian Royal Exchange Assurance Group, reported on the effects of installing briefing groups.

> The Group had initially carried out a survey to identify the fields in which communication was least effective and what the problems were, and found that 'an overwhelming case emerged for the development and improvement of organised, disciplined, systematic face-to-face communication.'
>
> There were no hard and fast rules about what should be briefed, Mr. Bewes said. Briefings could include anything from changes in working arrangements to discussion on results, expenses or the annual report.
>
> The benefits that the briefing groups approach brought, said Mr. Bewes, were savings in cash through improvement in decision-making, a higher level of staff commitment, improved relations between teams and their leaders, and a rapid feedback on policies and decisions.
>
> Supervisors gained confidence and increased respect from staff, and began to identify more closely with the management team. The staff got increased job satisfaction, higher morale and better relations with their superiors.

Incidentally the conference endorsed the primacy of face-to-face relationship of individuals over the written word. As the Lord Mayor of London, Sir Peter Studd, said 'It remains the most simple, straight-forward and honest method of communication.' Sir Henry Mance, Chairman of Lloyds, supported him. He believed that there were

> ...three tests to apply to any communication: the communication must be clear — it must mean the same thing to all who receive it and what the sender meant it to mean. It must be quick: communication that takes a long time to get down the line is likely to be highly dangerous. Third, there must be a response: 'It is interesting,' Sir Henry said, 'that in business dealings we expect, and generally get, a response to every communication even though it be only an acknowledgement for a cheque; but in staff matters we are very often content to put a notice on the board and leave it at that'.
>
> But the one single underlying feature of communication, Sir Henry added, was that it involved a relationship between two

parties, and basically between individual people. 'It is no accident that for hundreds of years the basic method of transacting business in markets has been by face-to-face confrontation between principals subsequently ratified by written contract, because by this method one can achieve the three criteria of good communication... It is personal contact and relationships which count, and the market system would not operate without it.'

JOINT CONSULTATION

Decisions in any group or organization must be taken by the leader and the members in varying proportions amongst themselves, depending upon the situation, the knowledge of the subordinates, the nature of the decision and the philosophy of the organization. Having already discussed these factors in *Training for Decisions* I shall not enlarge upon them here. Sufficient to recall that the more people share in decisions which affect their working lives the more they are inwardly moved to carry them out. Enthusiasm, involvement, commitment, a sense of responsibility: all these are strengthened by participating in the process of decision-making. Although the final decision may rest elsewhere, and may turn out to be other than an individual member would have desired, the fact that his voice has been heard-and-listened-to is a positive incentive in itself.

Consequently there is a solid case for meetings where the main emphasis is upon upwards communication. Three possible aims for such consultative or representative meetings have been succinctly defined by John Garnett:

— to give employees a chance to improve decisions by contributing comments before decisions are made;
— to make the fullest possible use of their experience and ideas in the efficient running of the enterprise;
— to give management and employees the opportunity to understand each other's views and objectives. [3]

Characteristically these are meetings where discussion takes place on any matter influencing the effectiveness or efficiency of the enterprise prior to decisions being made. Sometimes the group's views will be passed upwards; sometimes the decision will be made by the manager or supervisor on the spot and in the presence of those who have contributed to his judgement.

Consultative meetings may be distinguished from formal management/union discussions on such topics as wage systems, job evaluation, hours of work, holidays and holiday pay. In the latter instance elected representatives of work people in trade unions are seeking to reach formal agreement on matters relating to the 'individual needs' circle in the trefoil or three-circles model on p. 50. In consultations the active working members of an organization are being asked to contribute towards decisions mainly in the field of the common purpose, aims and objectives, and the shape of the structural organization necessary to achieve those short- and long-term ends. As the circles over-lap it is not always possible in practice to separate matters of concern for trade unions from those which belong to the individual as a member of a particular organization. But there is a distinction, and it is worth bearing it in mind.

It is usually assumed that a consultative group, formalized into a consultative committee, should exist on a factory or plant basis, although in very large organizations there may be a case for regional, national or international councils. Normally one might find one joint consultation committee, consisting of representatives from management and shop floor, in a factory employing perhaps 1,000 men and women or more. Thus it would act as a forum of debate, rather than as a cabinet for decision. Except in schemes for industrial democracy, where the committee becomes the governing council, the final decisions and the ultimate accountability will still rest with the board of directors.

Personally I think that the formally elected 'constitutional' consultative system needs to be supplemented by the flexible use of briefing groups in a secondary role as consultative groups, engaging in such activities as discussion, problem-solving and creative thinking. So that at some briefing meetings as much as two-thirds of the time might be reserved for *upwards* consultation in all the various degrees or shades of that word. The formal consultative meeting or committee has a 'safety net' role to play, especially where for some reason there is a majority or significant minority of non-union members. But we should expect to see its importance declining as the quality of leadership in working groups improves, the membership of white-collar unions grows, and the actual concerns of trade unions reach out beyond their present pre-occupations with pay, hours, safety and job security.

COMMITTEES

Committees have come under such heavy fire in recent years that it is worth recalling that in their heyday between 1900 and 1939 they were hailed by industry with as much enthusiasm as briefing groups are today. From the turn of the century they have inspired much faith as a method for running large organizations with the maximum involvement of individuals and departments.

The reasons for their present disfavour include the identification of committees with a particular method of making decisions by majority vote or consensus. They are associated with the institutions of democracy, in that Parliament does much of its work through committees, such as the Committee of Ways and Means, and has done so for centuries. Bodies which set out to copy Parliament, such as church synods and county councils, also adopted the committee method as one means of bridging the gap between the legislative and executive functions.

The emphasis upon individual accountability and the growing appreciation of the necessarily undemocratic (but not anti-democratic) nature of most working organizations, have drastically affected the image of committees. They are seen often as time-consuming chores. Yet the board of directors is a committee, and it often needs to appoint sub-committees. Contrary to the prevailing orthodoxy it is necessary to assert with Albert Sloan that large organizations cannot run without committees, in the general defined sense of 'a body of persons appointed or elected for some special business or function.'

The part played by committees in the total decision-making activity of an organization depends upon the purpose, structure and ethos of that organization, and discussion of it lies outside the present scope of this book. But committees do have an important function in communication which is neither primarily downwards (briefing) or upwards (consultative) but *sideways* or lateral.

This aspect of communication becomes especially important in large organizations, where individuals, departments or divisions are separated by large distances. Upwards and downwards communication may be taking place perfectly well, but it is also necessary for lateral discussions to happen as well. The mixed history of 'combined operations' between army, navy and air force amply illustrates how essential is the work of communicating for *co-ordination*. For besides being subordinates we are also co-ordinates one with another.

HOUSE JOURNALS AND SURVEYS
Letters, memoranda, reports and the like, follow the main trade routes of communication — upwards, downwards and sideways. Sometimes they travel the channels alone; at other times they act in concert with the spoken word. Their contents do not concern us here. For, to revert to the railway analogy, it is the network of tracks that we are

considering, not the type of train which is travelling on them. Company magazines, bulletins or news letters, however, providing they appear at regular intervals do merit attention, because they form another distinct line of communication.

Usually companies pay for most of the costs of their magazines and it is therefore not surprising that in the past they should be seen mainly as promoting downwards and sideways communication. In terms of the priority circles, the MUST and the better part of the SHOULD areas ought to be covered by personal encounters or small group meetings along the 'chain of command'. But that leaves the SHOULD—MIGHT shades to be conveyed by such means as bulletins, notice boards, news letters or house journals. This paperwork will be enhanced by illustrations, photographs and diagrams. In the future they may be increasingly supplemented by films or closed-circuit television pro-grammes. We cannot help being interested by the people we work with or for, and such methods help us to understand the personal and social nature of our organization, however vast. Fortunately there are plenty of examples of good company journals and much sound advice on producing them.[4]

Magazines are much less good at present as lines of communication for 'up' trains. Some journalists have hinted at Machiavellian (in the worst sense) practices by management to prevent or smother letters of complaint. For example, Vincent Hanna, writing in the *Sunday Times* in October 1971, was not enthusiastic about the correspondence column in the magazine of a large international computer firm:

> Frankly it isn't very impressive. Grievances are never presented in a way that could turn them into 'issues' capable of group discussion, and they are set along-side news stories in an attempt to make workers read unpopular sections of the journal. But it does enable management to pay lip service to the idea of grievance airing in public.[5]

On the other hand it could be argued that correspondence columns are an inefficient method of getting grievances righted. First, it is a slow process. There is nothing so sapping in interest as watching a slow-motion debate about the price of British Rail tea conducted in the correspondence columns of the daily newspapers, let alone in monthly journals. Secondly, a minor point becomes a great *cause celèbre* by publicizing it to perhaps 300,000 employees, and the spirit of discontent is contagious. The pen may be mightier than the sword, but the printed letter is as slow and cumbersome as a medieval battering ram.

There are other methods of uncovering complaints as well as positive suggestions. The consultative meeting should be the place where people feel free enough to raise what appear to be critical points. Such a setting has the advantage that others present can confirm or refute the universality of the complaint — is it *all* washrooms which are dirty, or only those in the painting shop?

The correspondence column does give the opportunity for anonymous letters. These are the cousins of 'poison pen' letters, and frequently suggest a lack of moral courage. On the other hand, a natural reticence at hurting people's feelings or jeopardizing a working relationship may drive us to take refuge behind a pseudonym. One more effective method of locating and releasing these critical but unassertive opinions is the *survey*.

For example, IBM conduct an annual opinion poll or attitude survey at each plant. Vincent Hanna and the *Sunday Times* checked the survey at the IBM factory at Havant with one of their own, and judged it to be fair.

There is the annual opinion poll taken at each plant. This is published and circularized among workers in a shortened form. Basically it deals with all aspects of IBM work and the satisfaction it produces. I was given access to the survey conducted last year at Havant, and found it accurate and fair as judged by my own researches.

It did reveal, however, one clear area for potential trouble; 46% of the workers stated that they did not receive enough formal training in their jobs.

There are some indications that the main area of dissatisfaction lies among the IBM non-graduate workers. 'We feel as if we are the drones in the system,' was how one technician put it to me, 'the best jobs are reserved for the graduate trainees, and the prospects for the others are less bright.'

One thing you learn very quickly about IBM management — it is adaptable. With the forewarnings built into its communication system, the company can anticipate trouble at the source and change policy before the snags manifest themselves.

Between 1962 and 1968 IBM carried out twenty-six surveys either in specific locations or special job groups. In 1968 four international surveys took place in sixteen countries in job groups. The following year a survey in six countries, backed by interviews and monitored by behavioural scientists, set out to explore the morale of the various national companies, with the following objectives:

> to identify matters requiring attention;
> to establish some way of measuring morale and its *trend*. (This is difficult to quantify but trends can be measured positively or negatively);
> to provide vital data for personnel planning;
> to provide information for management training to illustrate what employees expect — this is better than quoting Drucker etc;
> It is in itself a positive morale builder in that it indicates that the management takes the subject seriously;
> It provides powerful justification for management's action;
> It provides a measure of management performance. Employees are asked for opinions on their managers and the trends of these opinions are of great interest; they lead to improvement in performance as a result of the objective advice of the behavioural scientist.

The method of running these surveys follows three stages: announcement; group interviews to establish the subject matter uppermost in employees' minds; similar interviews to list the concerns of management. The consultant develops the questionnaire, which is in the form of choosing one of four possible answers to each question — this is to simplify analysis, but, as it may also frustrate, there are spare pages for any who wish to raise other subjects. All reports are voluntary and anonymous, but the results are fed back to all concerned. Postal surveys usually get 90% response, surveys in a particular shop usually get 99% response.

Although expensive in terms of time and money, surveys do have a part to play in the life of large organizations. But, like all public opinion polls, their interpretation requires specialist knowledge — and some pinches of salt.

THE GRAPE-VINE

Informality is one of the keynotes of our age. It conjures up a picture of relaxed ease, and a brave dispensing with all pompous and rigid formalities. But its history cannot support this edifice of value judgement. Indeed when Shakespeare wrote of 'these poore informall women' he probably meant that they were disordered in mind. Rather unflatteringly, the dictionary defines *informal* as, 'not done or made according to a regular or prescribed form; not observing forms; not according to order; irregular; unofficial, disorderly.'

It is common knowledge that alongside the network of official or regular lines and junctions of communication there exists an unofficial or informal exchange of ideas or information. The unreliability of this method is notorious. Indeed, during the American Civil War a 'despatch by grape-vine telegraph' – later shortened to 'grape-vine' – meant an extravagant or absurd story circulated as a hoax, or a false report.[6]

Passing any message from person to person is liable to lead to distortion, even if only two people are involved, as the following examples[7] of secretarial errors illustrate:

WHAT THE MANAGER SAID:	WHAT THE SECRETARY TYPED:
I can *heartily* reciprocate your good wishes.	I can *hardly* reciprocate your good wishes.
It is not wise to *mix* type *faces.*	It is not wise to *skip* type *spaces.*
He *acceded to* these restrictions.	He *exceeded* these restrictions.
Archimedes said...	*Our committees* said...
This will *enable* us to close the contract.	This will *unable* us to close the contract.

The more people in the lines of communication the more the content tends to lose its shape. In a legendary trench on the Western Front during the First World War a colonel asked his men to pass down the line an oral message to the neighbouring regiment a mile away, which said: 'Send reinforcements – we are going to advance.' At the time the message had been exchanged by three hundred cold and wet soldiers manning the trench it had become: 'Send three-and-four-pence – we are going to a dance.'

Thus informal communication allows rumours to snowball especially if they contain threats to individual needs and hopes. Bad news travels fast. For these reasons managers have traditionally looked upon the factory grape-vine with a suspicion amounting to hostility, over-looking the fact that they have their own grape-vines and 'old-boy nets' But these informal contacts should be positively welcomed as a valuable 'alternative system' to the formal system of communications. In other words, the grape-vine ought to give upwards feedback on how well the main channels of communication are working, and whether or not they are carrying the information which is necessary in the situation.

Secondly, the grape-vine can bear good news as well as bad. Truth can leap along its branches, especially when the 'official channels' are clogged thick with green slime and mud. Sometimes leaders can choose to send messages along the grape-vine, or relay them through those who use that medium most. Only good coins will drive out a debased money. Rumour originally meant a widespread report of a *favourable* or *complimentary* nature, and it only came later to have its more neutral tone, as general talk or hearsay not based upon definite knowledge or clear evidence circulating in a community. Obviously the better rumours are those which act as advance-guards preparing the way for good news. The only way to scotch or control bad rumours is to produce the knowledge or evidence, or the reasons why it is not available, and explain the general policies of the organization in that field. But this work should be done through the normal and formal system, not through a series of 'crisis' meetings.

Any organization needs much informal exchange of ideas and opinions upwards and downwards, and no system of communication has yet been invented which can bear all the growing volume of that legitimate traffic. We shall always need the coffee breaks, lunch meetings and conversations on the train. What we hear between the words, and what we project non-verbally in confidence or anxiety is as much part of the total communications in an organization as the briefing group or the company telephone system.

These informal contacts are especially important for lateral communication. It is perhaps salutary for those of us engaged in management training to reflect on the fact that a major value for the participants in staff-college courses, and in-company and in-service programmes lies precisely in the opportunity such get-togethers provide for the exchange of ideas and attitudes, names and jobs on the sideways or lateral-communication dual carriageway. Relationships forged at such times facilitate the intercourse of information by hook or by crook. Of course bad leaders always fear their subordinates getting together to compare notes, because they fear the exposure of their own incompetence and because they entertain a low view of human nature anyway. Fortunately the number of organizations with such helmsmen at the tiller is dwindling rapidly.

On the whole the informal grape-vine bears the spoken word; indeed, rumour derives from the Latin word for voice. But the printing press can serve the grape-vine as well. As organizations become larger and as the social conscience of their members flexes its muscles, we should expect to see the growth of unofficial news sheets or industrial journals which offer a mixture of rumour and gossip, complaints and challenge to the apparent values of the organization. Charles Foley, writing in *The Observer* in February 1972, reported as much from San Francisco:

> A new species of underground newspaper is being spawned in the western offices of several giant United States companies. Discontented employees who traditionally resort to the nearest bar to curse the boss are now snatching up copies of weeklies and monthlies that blast away at a dozen major firms.
>
> Boardrooms are raked with the grapeshot of gossip and satire; nothing is sacred — from the managerial menu to the company product, for that matter, the whole corporate system. What hurts still more is that many of the under-ground editors and writers are young, socially aware people of the kind big companies have been trying to attract. They joined the system with silent reservations — and have since found reason for their doubts.
>
> San Francisco — the ever-experimental city — has the largest number of rebel papers. The huge Metropolitan Life Insurance has the Met Lifer; Pacific Telephone and Telegraph the At and T Express; telephone operators across the bay in Oakland publish the Operating Underground; and a famous East Bay cannery puts out Can You Dig It? which attacks racism in hiring and promotion, working conditions and the wage freeze.
>
> The Met Lifer, run by ex-student activists, began with attacks on political and social issues, including the Indo-China war. The company was accused of using computers made by Honeywell Inc., which has supplied fragmentation bombs for Vietnam.
>
> The paper has sold better with job complaints and scored heavily with a campaign against the three different lunches offered to the insurance company's 1,700 workers. These varied from plain frankfurters for the proletariat to grilled perch and veal cutlets in the executive dining room for those not on diet for overweight or ulcers. Today everyone eats the same food.

Conclusion

Besides the hierarchical structure of rules, which acts as the primary communication framework, the large organization needs other methods. The shape or form which these take will vary according to the kind of organization, but we can identify them as Briefing Groups, Joint Consultation, Committees, News Sheets and Surveys, and the

Grape-vine. In the anatomy of communication each of these deserve careful study, for they have a vital part to play in the over-all health of the organization. Owing to their poor communication systems the dinosaurs became extinct. No one system is necessarily right for all organizations. What is important, however, is that the methods making up the present system as appropriate to the needs of a given enterprise should be understood, maintained, modified where necessary. So vital is this necessity that the Industrial Relations Code of Practice can conclude: 'Management, employee representatives and trade unions should co-operate in ensuring that effective communication and consultation take place.'

General Eisenhower at Work:
A Case Study in Organizational Communication

'In its day-to-day conduct of business, management needs both to give information to employees and to receive information from them. Effective arrangements should be made to facilitate this two-way flow. The most important method of communication is by word of mouth, through personal contact between each manager and his immediate employees, and between managers and employee representatives.'

These words from the Code of Practice are not merely speculations, for there is much evidence to support the primacy of two-way oral communication. In the Second World War the allied leaders realized the value of talking directly with the troops, a lesson which many senior managers have yet to learn. General Eisenhower later wrote:

At times I received advice from friends, urging me to give up or curtail visits to troops. They correctly stated that, so far as the mass of men was concerned, I could never speak, personally, to more than a tiny percentage. They argued, therefore, that I was merely wearing myself out, without accomplishing anything significant, so far as the whole Army was concerned. With this I did not agree. In the first place I felt that through constant talking to enlisted men I gained accurate impressions of their state of mind. I talked to them about anything and everything: a favourite question of mine was to inquire whether the particular squad or platoon had figured out any new trick or gadget for use in infantry fighting. I would talk about anything so long as I could get the soldier to talk to me in return.

I knew, of course, that news of a visit with even a few men in a division would soon spread throughout the unit. This, I felt, would encourage men to talk to their superiors, and this habit, I believe, promotes efficiency. There is, among the mass of individuals who carry the rifles in war, a great amount of ingenuity and initiative. If men can naturally and without restraint talk to their officers, the products of their resourcefulness become available to all. Moreover, out of the habit grows mutual confidence, a feeling of partnership that is the essence of esprit de corps. An army fearful of its officers is never as good as one that trusts and confides in its leaders.

One day I had an appointment to meet five United States senators. As they walked into my office I received a telegram from a staff officer, stating that a newspaper article alleged the existence at the Lucky Strike camp of intolerable conditions. The story said that men were crowded together, were improperly fed, lived under unsanitary conditions, and were treated with an entire lack of sympathy and understanding. The policy was exactly the opposite. Automatic furloughs to the States had been approved for all liberated Americans and we had assigned specially selected officers to care for them.

Even if the report should prove partially true it represented a very definite failure to carry out strict orders somewhere along the line. I determined to go see for myself and told my pilot to get my plane ready for instant departure. I turned to the five senators, apologized for my inability to keep my appointment, and explained why it was necessary for me to depart instantly for Lucky Strike. I told them, however, that if they desired to talk with me they could accompany me on the trip. I pointed out that at Lucky Strike they would have a chance to visit with thousands of recovered prisoners of war and that at no other place could they find such a concentration of American citizens. They all accepted with alacrity.

In less than two hours we arrived at Lucky Strike and started our inspection. We roamed around the camp and found no basis for the startling statements made in the disturbing telegram. There were only two points concerning which our men exhibited any impatience. The first of these was the food. It was of good quality and well cooked but the doctors would not permit salt, pepper, or any kind of seasoning to be used because they were considered damaging to men who had undergone virtual starvation over periods ranging from weeks to years. The senators and I had dinner with the men and we agreed that a completely unseasoned diet was lacking in taste appeal. However, it was a technical point on which I did not feel capable of challenging the doctors.

The other understandable complaint was the length of time that men were compelled to stay in the camp before securing transportation to America. This was owing to lack of ships. Freighters, which constituted the vast proportion of our overseas transport service at that stage of the war, were not suited for transportation of passengers. These ships lacked facilities for providing drinking water, while toilet and other sanitary provisions were normally adequate only for the crew. The men did not know these things and it angered them to see ships leaving the harbor virtually empty when they were so anxious to go home.

So pleased did the soldiers seem to be by our visit that they followed us around the camp by the hundreds. When we finally returned to the airplane we found that an enterprising group had installed a loudspeaker system, with the microphone at the door of my plane. A committee of sergeants came up and rather diffidently said that the men would like to see and hear the commanding general. There were some fifteen to twenty thousand in the crowd around the plane.

In hundreds of places under almost every kind of war condition I had talked to American soldiers, both individually and in groups up to the size of a division. But on that occasion I was momentarily at a loss for something to say. Every one of those present had undergone privation beyond the imagination of the normal human. It seemed futile to attempt, out of my own experience, to say anything that could possibly appeal to such an enormous acaccumulation of knowledge of suffering.

Then I had a happy thought. It was an idea for speeding up the return of these men to the homeland. So I took the microphone and told the assembled multitude there were two methods by which they could go home. The first of these was to load on every returning troop-ship the maximum number for which the ship was designed. This was current practice.

Then I suggested that, since submarines were no longer a menace, we could place on each of these returning ships double the normal capacity, but that this would require one man to sleep in the daytime so that another soldier could have his bunk during the night. It would also compel congestion and inconvenience everywhere on the ship. I asked the crowd which one of the two schemes they would prefer me to follow. The roar of approval for the double-loading plan left no doubt as to their desires.

When the noise had subsided I said to them: 'Very well, that's the way we shall do it. But I must warn you men that there are five United States senators accompanying me today. Consequently when you get home it is going to do you no good to write letters to the papers or to your senator complaining about overcrowding on returning ships. You have made your own choice and so now you will have to like it.'

The shout of laughter that went up left no doubt that the men were completely happy with their choice. I never afterward heard of a single complaint voiced by one of them because of discomfort on the homeward journey.

CHAPTER FIVE

EFFECTIVE SPEAKING

Speak properly, and in as few words as you can, but
always plainly; for the end of speech is not
ostentation, but to be understood.

WILLIAM PENN

Occasions for public speaking abound. In our working lives we may
have to give briefings or talks, take part in presentations or even deliver
formal lectures. Some occupations — notably law, politics and
education — make heavy demands on the speaking abilities of their
members. Others, including the managerial and supervisory professions,
are beginning to share this characteristic as the art of communication
becomes ever more essential for getting results through working with
people.

In industry, commerce and the public services, however, the
occasions for public speaking may be less formal — a few words before
a meeting, a question to a committee, a briefing to initiate a special
job — but these times call for effective speech from the manager or
leader.

Nor should the scope of this chapter be limited entirely to the
workaday world. Most of us live in communities; all of us belong to
families or have friends. We may never launch a ship or open a bazaar,
but few of us can avoid being asked 'to say a few words' at some stage
or another in our lives. Our words may enhance the occasion, like a
good speech at a wedding. Or our contribution may sway a meeting of a
society or neighbourhood association. At work and in the local
community the ability to communicate or speak well is inextricably
bound up with good leadership and good membership.

The Search for Rules

So important is public speaking that it would be surprising if a great
deal of ink had not been spilt on the subject. The earliest writer on
'rhetoric', or the art of using language so as to instruct, move or delight
others, is said to have been a Sicilian called Corax in the 460s B.C., but
unfortunately his treatise has not survived. In the following centuries

such practitioners as Demosthenes in Athens and Cicero in Rome brought 'rhetoric' to a high pitch of excellence according to the standards and expectations of their day. A study of their 'word skills' and writings, along with the efforts of the smaller fry of professional orators, formed the basis for later attempts at formulating the rules of 'the art of persuasion', as Aristotle called it in his own book — *Rhetoric*.

Perhaps the best way to get the flavour of this passionate search for rules is to take the most complete account of the art of oratory as our framework — Quintilian's *Institutio Oratoria*, written about 95 A.D., when the Roman Empire was nearing its zenith. Like Caesar with Gaul he found his subject to be divided into three parts: the art of rhetoric, the speech itself and the situation that calls it forth.

Quintilian gave most attention to 'the art of rhetoric', which in turn he placed in five divisions. The first two he called 'invention' (collecting the material) and 'disposition' (arranging it in order). Then came the labour of putting it all into words, memorizing it, and finally, delivering the finished speech. The speech itself should also have five phases: an introduction to gain the goodwill of the audience; a statement of the point at issue; arguments to prove your case; refutations of contrary arguments; and then a conclusion (peroration) which either re-capitulated the main points or else appealed to the audience's emotions.

It was the third part of the art of rhetoric, the putting it into words, which received the most attention from Quintilian and other writers. They called this 'elocution', from the Latin verb 'to speak out'. For the Romans this meant roughly the same as our word 'style': only later did it arrive at its modern use, which virtually limits it to pronunciation. Style covered all the skills and tricks of constructing phrases and sentences so as to serve the content in hand and please the audience.

From the earliest times we can trace the tension between content and method, the Lion and the Unicorn of language, in the disputes of the rhetoricians. One school, the 'Asians', favoured a flowery and elaborate style, with plenty of verbal fireworks thrown in for fun. The other school, the 'Atticists' advocated a plain and unadorned 'elocution'. Allowing the content to speak for itself, they frowned on unnecessary frills. In architecture we may trace the same developments made visible: the ornate splendours of baroque on the one hand contrasting with the more austere line and proportion of classic Greek and Roman buildings on the other hand.

Demosthenes never added stylistic ornaments to embellish his own speeches but he kept the audience on the edge of their seats with a variety of devices: paradoxical arguments, dramatic outbursts, imaginary dialogues, the repetition of salient points and a wit which could be crude, scurrilous and bitter. But his language was simple, at times colloquial. Cicero, almost two centuries later, blended the Attic and Asian approaches. He was a master of the long, rolling, 'periodic' sentences, which he could break out upon the shores of his audiences' minds. When he was summoning up anger against his political opponents his sentences could sound clipped and staccato, like arrows rattling ferociously on a shield. While Cicero never lost sight of the immediate essential – the point he wanted to make – he could align words with such a fine ear that they sounded like poetry. Indeed we are told that on occasion, when he uttered a particular combination of syllables at the end of a sentence, the audience would leap to their feet in tumultuous applause.

By considering the third and last general category in Quintilian's treatise – the kind of speech – we can see the weakness in this whole attempt to construct a science of rhetoric or oratory. Quintilian recognized three main types of speech to which his rules would apply: show speeches (which he called 'demonstrative' ones), political or 'deliberative' ones, and legal pleadings. We only have to reflect that perhaps the greatest speech of all time, the Sermon on the Mount, delivered not a dozen years before Quintilian's birth, does not fit any of these categories, to realize how many kinds of speaking are left out of the traditional classification. As the centuries passed these limitations became more apparent. Rhetoric became backward-looking; it ossified by failing to adapt to the changing situation and the consequent needs of practical men. From politics and public life the concept of rhetoric retreated into the law courts and academies. It became increasingly identified with form (or methods) rather than content, with the mannerisms of speech and gesture which owe more to the Asians than the Atticists. Not only the kinds of speeches but also the audiences changed, and these alterations rendered the more static corpus of books on rhetoric out-of-date. The same is true for modern manuals on public speaking in our own dynamic world. Even Winston Churchill's oratory now sounds a little dated.

Yet the thoughts of the Greek and Roman masters on the six elements of human communication – the points and centre of the star described in Chapter Two – are well worth attending to. For example, they never saw public speaking as a mere string of techniques, gimmicks or tricks of persuasion. They focused attention upon the moral as well as the intellectual and educational gifts of the communicator. As Cato said, a true orator is 'a good man skilled in speaking'. The integrity and kindliness of Quintilian still shines through his pages.

Secondly, the Greek and Roman masters were aware of the importance of the content: they knew that truth or justice communicates better than lies or evil. Of course they knew also that a skilful speaker could cause an untruth or injustice to be accepted, and some believed that the good of the state sometimes justified such advocacy. But they recognized this as being in some way an inversion of the natural order. Values such as goodness, happiness, justice, and moderation were the 'places' where arguments could be found. One word – 'topics' – comes from the Greek word for 'places' used by Aristotle in this way.

Thirdly, the traditional theorists of ancient times stressed the advantages of knowing your audience, and that remains equally valid today. They were especially interested in the psychology of emotions, such as anger or pity. In our own times, when we have witnessed the effects of the emotion-arousing oratory of Hitler and Mussolini, and at a cultural phase when if anything we rather distrust emotional displays, this aspect of knowing people may not greatly appeal to us. But it is the abiding message of the past great masters that a thorough knowledge of people in general and the audience in particular is essential if the aims of public speaking are to be achieved. In the terse words of Cicero these aims are *docere, movere, delectare*: to instruct, to move and to delight.

Five Principles of Good Speaking

Should we abandon the search for principles or rules and rely upon the mind's general thinking abilities of analysing, synthesizing and valuing? For two reasons I do not think so. First, the gap between our mind's general faculties and the highly specific actual situations of speaking aloud to one or more people is too wide: we need some bridges across it, some ready-made shapes into which these abilities can flow. Merely to tell someone to analyse (content, audience, and situation) and synthesize (content with methods) is not enough. Such advice would be too general. Secondly, although each communication is unique – unlike any before or after – to some extent they can be grouped into families. The wedding speech situation, for example, has a habit of cropping up repeatedly. Thus it should be possible to make some generalizations.

But what sort of generalizations? Rules come in assorted sizes and shapes. 'Love your neighbour' is qualitatively different from 'Brush your teeth after meals'. The danger of being too specific is that you ignore the situational variables. The rule then has the advantage of being concrete and practical, but it accumulates a 'tail' of 'ifs' and 'buts'. As the months pass it can die the proverbial death of a thousand qualifications. If, on the other hand, the rules are too general they become too abstract, and the mind cannot get a purchase on them. We may agree but we do not buy them in the auction of practical ideas. 'Think!' may be a good rule, but it does not help very much.

The answer may lie in the identification of the appropriate values. Values come in different galaxies and clusters. Where communication is concerned we need to be able to call into play a certain family of values, so that they intermingle with the intellectual and practical work of analysing and synthesizing content, methods, communicants and situation. Values are not victims to changes in fashion or to the whims of particular situations: they last. From the point of view of training it is essential that we build these values into our semiconscious or depth minds. We can best do this by a conscious phase when we treat the values in question as principles or rules. Verbally we can express this harnessing of will-o'-the-wisp values by prefixing each with the imperative 'Be'. An additional advantage of changing values into principles, or seeing them as the primary rules, is that we can use them for evaluating communication as well as for shaping it.

BE PREPARED

In a sense this principle covers all our working life: it is an expression of practical wisdom. As such the praises of its virtues or value have been sung throughout history. Most of us, for example, can recall the Parable of the Wise and Foolish Virgins. The possibility of preparation springs from our endowment with foresight and imagination: because we can see ahead we can also prepare for what is to come.

Our immediate preparations in speaking will focus on collecting, surveying and arranging our material, finding out about the communicants or receivers and considering the situation. They will usually include making a *plan* of the communication, be it long or short. This may be on paper: an outline of the main phases or stages of a speech or lecture, annotated with the illustrations or examples used to buttress the salient points. Or the plan may be constructed in one's head, using the Communication Star, if time does not allow for even an outline on the back of an envelope.

The bare essentials of the plan are the identification of the central *aim* or *objective* of the communication — what you really want to say — the arrangement of the material to this end, and the 'methods of instruction' to be employed. It is vital to have some sort of plan. By itself a good plan – one that satisfactorily promises to achieve its end – does not guarantee success, but not having any plan can virtually guarantee failure.

There are no particular rules for such plans, except the suggestion that formal speeches should include a *beginning, middle* and *end.* Cicero ignored the complicated rules of structure current in his day, but his speeches always contained an introduction, some sort of main body and a concluding peroration. A good meal, as opposed to a snack, should consist of a 'starter', an entrée and a sweet. Apart from the general principle that the material should be so presented as to fulfil the objective, the three-point programme of beginning, middle and end is worth keeping in mind.

Thorough preparation should also include a visit to the scene of the crime, and a meeting with those whom one is to talk to. Situations are so varied, however, that this is not always necessary: one may know the room and the people extremely well. If not, however, it is essential to reconnoitre the place, checking the seating arrangements, lighting and acoustics, potential external or internal distractions, and any equipment which is being supplied for your use. You should not be satisfied until you (or someone you trust) have seen the equipment in question working. In my experience the things that can go wrong with film projectors, tape recorders, closed-circuit television, and overhead projectors are legion. 'I'm sorry, I am not used to this particular model', hisses the operator apologetically as the machine breaks down. But it is the communicator who carries the responsibility: he has already communicated to his audience that he has failed to observe the first principle: Be Prepared. Of course, you will gain marks if you show unflappability, or even fish out the odd spare part from your pocket – but who wants to live dangerously?

John Casson makes this point well in his description of 'setting the stage'. Of course most speakers have to be their own stage-managers, but the advice holds good when applied to oneself:

In a theatre, stage-management is the organising of mechanics of effective presentation. It includes setting the stage, lighting it, providing the right properties at the right time and in the right place. The stage-manager's job is so to manage all these mechanics that the actor doesn't have to think about them or be distracted by the lack of them. If anything goes seriously wrong every member of the audience is going to see it and there is no possible way in which the stage-manager could explain why it has gone wrong or to justify its going wrong. It had just gone wrong and from that moment it is irretrievable in the minds of the audience. If something happens for which he feels he needs to apologise, or should apologise, then he has failed. A good stage-manager's attitude of mind is therefore at all times one of using his imagination to anticipate every conceivable disaster that could or might occur. He does it by mentally going through every operation that every actor and every member of the stage staff might have to perform, and checks to see that everything has been done to see that the operation can be performed as easily and as safely as possible. It's his job to see that nothing happens that will distract actors and audience from their close interaction with each other.[1]

Planning and the material advance preparations necessary to implement the plan are the immediate or tactical applications of the Be Prepared principle. They transform raw meat into a tender, succulent and garnished dish, set on a clean warm plate on an attractively laid out table. By good preparations we also make it easier for our guests to enjoy the common meal. But there are also the more strategic or longer-term applications of the principle. All education and training should be preparing us to communicate more effectively. Training refers to skills and techniques; education signifies the stocking of our depth minds with potentially relevant ideas, facts, experiences, pictures and information.

The depth mind, however, like the sea does not always disgorge its treasures at our command. For those who must speak often, either in formal settings or else in committees and discussions, it is a good idea to keep a filing system or perhaps a *common place book*, an ordinary notebook in which one records ideas, thoughts, illustrations, jests or newspaper cuttings – anything which might prove to be useful. To extend its usefulness, make it also a record of *lessons* in communication: your own observations on what works and what does not, along with the tips and rules of thumb which come your way. As well as the value of the contents in what will be your own book on communication, this method keeps the mind constantly preparing for the sudden short moments of speaking. This preparation should be a continuous process.

Time is often in short supply for preparations, but it is rare to find yourself without even a minute to make a plan. Such crisis occasions do have the advantage of revealing the person who is more-or-less always ready to speak in certain areas if called upon to do so. But the good communicator seeks to avoid these surprises.

In summary: the principle of Be Prepared should be applied specifically by making some sort of workable plan for the speech or talk, one which at least fully covers the main points you want to make. The traditional framework of beginning, middle and end is a good start, although the time available may compel us even to chop down this skeleton. Secondly, no one is prepared until the materials, setting and administrative details have been made ready, checked or settled. Thirdly, Be Prepared should govern our long-term work: the slow and unhurried mastery of our aims and subject, all the relevant background knowledge, the skills and methods of instruction or dialogue, and understanding of people's needs and wants. Lastly, preparation should encompass our own selves − the personality which must refract the light of even the most faint truth, the less obvious aspects of our life which will communicate whatever cosmetics we paint on to disguise them. Can they be changed? Yes, of course they can, but only over a longish period of time.

BE CLEAR

Clarity is the quality of being unclouded or transparent. A clear sky is one free of clouds, mists and haze. With reference to speech it means free from any confusion and hence easy to understand.

Being clear is not primarily a matter of sentences and words. The value of clarity is an inner one: it should act as a principle, purifying thought at its source, in the mind. Clear thinking issues in a clear utterance: if one's ideas or theories are basically muddy or muddled, then it will be a miracle if the external communication of them is easily understood. Thus the application of this principle begins a long way back from the board room or executive office, in the struggle to achieve a piece of clarity in the uncertain weather of the mind. This entails mastering the intellectual skills of analysing, synthesizing and valuing.[2]

It should not be supposed that what is clear is automatically true. Someone once said that George Bernard Shaw's head contained a confusion of clear ideas. Be that as it may, truth does not always come purified and translucent, and 'all that glitters is not gold'. Clarity is a mercenary value: it serves well whoever is prepared to pay the price for it. That price includes the willingness to suffer muddled confusion before the clouds part, the dust settles and the issue, problem or course of action becomes crystal clear. If it becomes a matter of communicating to others, the combination of truth and clarity is well-nigh irresistible, certainly so in the long run.

One of the masters of our time in applying the principle of Be Clear was Field-Marshal Montgomery. His wartime 'briefings' became a legend for those who heard him. As a boy at St Paul's School in 1947 I heard Lord Montgomery when he returned to his old school to describe his D-Day plans. It was the building he had used during the war as Allied Headquarters, indeed in the same lecture room he and the other generals had used for their final presentations to King George VI and Churchill, and so it was not difficult for a boy of fourteen years to capture the 'atmosphere', as Montgomery liked to call it. Above all his refreshing clarity lingers. Brigadier Essame emphasized it in his account of Montgomery at work:

> He could describe a complex situation with amazing lucidity and sum up a long exercise without the use of a single note. He looked straight into the eyes of the audience when he spoke. He had a remarkable flair for picking out the essence of a problem, and for indicating its solution with startling clarity. It was almost impossible to misunderstand his meaning, however unpalatable it might be. [3]

The principle of Be Clear needs to attack like sulphuric acid the corrosions which discolour the work of arrangement, reasoning and expression in our minds. The arrangement or structure of what you are saying should be clear, so that people know roughly where they are and where they are going. The reasoning should be sharp and clean cut, without the blurred edges of those who gloss over the issues. Above all the value dimension of the matter in hand should be clarified, for it is this realm which releases most mud into the pools of thought. Lastly, the principle of lucidity invites us to shun the obscure reference, the clouded remark, the allusion which few will understand, or the word which is fashionable but all too muddy in its meaning.

BE SIMPLE

The third principle – simplicity – is a first cousin to clarity. It means uncomplicated. Its cardinal importance for communication stems from the fact that our minds find it easier to take in what is simple. The simple is that which is composed of one substance, ingredient or element: it is not compounded or blended with 'foreign bodies' or unnecessary additions.

Again this principle should be applied to the fountain of our words, our minds and their thoughts. The search for simplicity in thinking is the same as the search for the essence of a subject, that which is specific to it and not composite or mixed up with other matters. Such a quest demands skills of analysing. We have to dissect, discard, blow and burn before we isolate the essential simplicity of a subject.

At this point we may fruitfully distinguish between being simple and being *simpliste* or simplistic. The French version we can use for those who present a complicated matter in the false clothes of a bogus simplicity. Oversimplification is not the same as being simple; simplicity should not be mistaken for simple-mindedness. To be simple requires a lot of hard work, especially if we have to present a subject which has many complications when studied in detail. But even if the subject is inherently complex we still have the choice to make between presenting its complexities in the simplest possible way, or reflecting the complications in both the arrangement of our talk and the language we employ. The ability to speak simply about difficult subjects – without oversimplification – is one of the marks of an effective speaker. We should certainly not fall into the trap of equating simplicity with superficiality. It is quite possible for the simple to have depth and the sophisticated to be empty.

In practical matters, where the desired result of communication is action, the more simple the instructions or plans the more likely people are to remember them and therefore carry them through. Writing to Lady Hamilton in October 1805 from HMS *Victory,* Nelson described the reaction of his captains to the strategy he outlined for the impending battle of Trafalgar:

> I joined the Fleet late on the evening of 28th of September, but could not communicate with them until the next morning. I believe that my arrival was most welcome, not only to the Commander of the Fleet, but also to every individual in it; and when I came to explain to them the *'Nelson touch'*, it was like an electric shock. Some shed tears, all approved – 'It was new – it was singular – it was simple!' and, from Admirals downwards, it was repeated – 'It must succeed, if ever they will allow us to get at them.'[4]

It is important, however, that the communicator should have been aware of all the difficulties and worked his way through the complexities to the heart of the matter, to the essential simplicity of the phenomena. This is as true for the scientist as for the military leader. Max Perutz, himself a Nobel Prize winner in chemistry, commentated on the capacity of Professor Sir Lawrence Bragg in this respect:

> His mind leaps like a prima ballerina, with perfect ease. What is so

unique about it — and this is what made his lectures so marvellous — is the combination of penetrating logic and visual imagery. Many of his successes in crystal structure analysis are due to this power of visualizing the aesthetically and physically most satisfying way of arranging a complicated set of atoms in space and then having found it, with a triumphant smile, he would prove the beauty and essential simplicity of the final solution.[5]

Wherever we look we find the same story: good speakers naturally apply the principle of Be Simple, and it is the less good ones who lose themselves and their audience in a maze of complications, real and imagined. Chancellor Willy Brandt of West Germany said of Jean Monnet, the father of the Common Market: 'He had the ability to put complicated matters into simple formulae.' Doubtless in politics simplicity is a sign of statesmanship just as it accompanies outstanding ability in the arts and sciences.

Apart from content and arrangement the principle of Be Simple should also be applied to language. Here we have to fight an endless battle against the thoughtless use of jargon in public conversation or speeches. But again the price of freedom from this particular piece of professional tyranny is the knowledge of the complications and ramifications which the trade vocabulary, signs and symbols have come to stand for. Otherwise the talk will be *simpliste*. Perhaps we have to earn the right to speak simply.

'I am allowed to use plain English because everybody knows that I could use mathematical logic if I chose', wrote Bertrand Russell in *Portraits from Memory*. 'I suggest to young professors that their first work be in a jargon only to be understood by the erudite few. With that behind them, they can ever after say what they have to say in a language "understanded" of the people.'[6] His advice applies equally well to all who have to speak to their fellow men about technical matters.

BE VIVID

The principle of vividness covers all that goes to make what we say interesting, arresting and attractive. From the Latin verb *vivere*, to live, the word vivid means literally 'full of life'. The characteristics it points to spring from the presence of young kicking life in both the speaker (whatever his age) and the subject: vigorous, active, enthusiastic, energetic, strong, warm, fresh, bright, brilliant and lively. When the subject or content is clear and simple it is already well on the road to becoming vivid, but we may still have to let it come to life.

Thus vividness is not something that can be lightly superimposed when all the other preparatory work is completed. Nor is it the result of giving one's personality full play to express itself, like a fountain playing in the sunlight. All public speaking, however slight the occasion should be 'truth *through* personality'. It is the truth which we have to vivify or bring to life for the other person, never ourselves. Only then can the speaker produce what the poet Thomas Gray called 'thoughts that breathe, and words that burn'.

The first application of the principle Be Vivid is to be interested in what one is talking about and the persons to whom one is talking – in that order. Interest, one of the forms of life itself, is a magnetic quality which is in people and not in subjects. It is true, of course, that genetic inheritance, family upbringing and education predispose us to being interested in certain subjects or topics rather than others. But these fields are as broad as the plains: people, things, ideas, the past, present or future. Within such expanses there are many camping grounds. Moreover, we share some common or universal traits, and if one human person is genuinely interested in some subject it will be surprising if he can find no one to share his interest.

Interest, however, can be a quiet and unassuming movement of the mind. We may acknowledge it in others, but not be necessarily moved to share it. Not all those who have an interest in what they wish to communicate also possess the gift of kindling interest in an audience. But we all find it hard to resist enthusiasm, which is interest blazing and crackling with happy flames. It is extremely difficult for an enthusiastic speaker to be dull: quite naturally he is applying the principle of Being Vivid.

Enthusiasm originally meant in the old Greek the quality of 'being invaded by the divine spirit'. As St Paul records, some of his spirit-possessed congregations babbled away incoherently, like drunkards filled with new wine. They were enthusiastic, but the spirit did not connect and flow into the ordinary language of the day: 'I would rather speak five intelligible words, for the benefit of others as well as myself, than thousands of words in the language of ecstasy', Paul assured his Corinthian readers. The problem for the enthusiast is often how to channel his surging 'ecstasy' into the five intelligible words. At least his face and voice should 'give him away'; they proclaim that – take it or leave it – he finds the subject interesting, even absorbing and fascinating. John Casson writes:

Enthusiasm consists of a permanent, intense delight in what is happening in the life around us at all times, combined with a passionate determination to create something from it, some order, some pattern, some artefacts, with gusto and delight. It means attacking problems, puzzles and obstacles with gumption and with relish.

We can develop this drive in ourselves by consciously looking for the enthralling, the exciting, the enchanting, the emotionally moving in even the most routine or most trivial matters, and applying ourselves to it and with all the vigour of which we are capable. We don't have to display a frenzy of histrionics and so become a menace to our friends. But we do need to enjoy unashamedly and uninhibitedly whatever we are doing.[7]

Beyond these essentials quite how you apply the principle of vividness depends upon your creative imagination and the characteristics of the other points of the Communication Star: the content, the methods available, the receivers and the situation. Where mass communications are involved, a theatrical sense for the 'drama' may be the way forward. Montgomery and Nelson both 'stage-managed' their communications. 'Monty', alone on the stage, tiers of coloured medal ribbons on his battledress, could communicate the inherent drama of battle. Nor was it perhaps just chance that Nelson loved a former actress, or that he insisted on donning his dress uniform of blue laced with gold on the fateful day of Trafalgar. Above all, he had the ability to capture a great moment and let it speak for itself, with all the flair of a great actor on the stage.

In smaller gatherings or groups and in less intrinsically dramatic situations the attempt to be dramatic can soon land us on the rocks of amateur theatricals. Thus the first step is always to look for *relevant* vividness in the subject. For example, I recall one afternoon's instruction in the Army on digging trenches. After a talk on the theory of it, we recruits were marched to the middle of a large field, given spades and told that in thirty minutes a machine gun would sweep the field with fire. None of us had ever dug so fast in our lives... It was a lesson on a fairly humdrum subject, but the instructor had discovered and released the vividness within it.

Thus vividness springs from the interest and enthusiasm in the mind and heart of the communicator. But it has to become visible in the methods and language which the communicator recruits for his purpose. Audio or visual aids can help a lot, yet they ought to remain *aids* for vividness, not substitutes for it. As we have seen, the structure

84

of the communication, or the order in which the content is presented, can induce vividness. The art here is so to arrange material that the form itself, not the ornaments or aids, convey the life-breath of interest and enthusiasm. Form includes not only the life-less structure of the talk or briefing as it lies inert on the planning-board, but the sense of proportion and timing which allows you to give the right emphasis to each part of the whole. Vividness is served if there is an effortless speed; it is destroyed by the two ugly sisters – Hurry and Worry. Thus, to quote again the advertisement for a famous make of motor-car, a communication should have 'Grace, Pace and Space'.

When the structure and timing is clear and the visual aids sorted out, there remains what could be called the tactics of vividness – the style or language of the speaker. Many textbooks at this point give long lists of figures of speech and idioms to avoid. My own difficulty with such lists is remembering them in heat and excitement when I am actually speaking. Fortunately the principles of Be Clear and Be Simple attack these porridge-like expressions, and they may be conveniently left until later for consideration in Chapter Seven. Here it remains for us to look at the heart of the matter when it comes to vivid speech, and that rests upon the fact that perhaps the majority of people have visual minds: they see things in pictures and not by hearing abstractions. Thus for the communicator, as Confucius said, *A picture is worth a thousand words.*

Best of all is the actual picture, plan or visual symbols supported by words; second best is the word picture. These come in various sizes, from the story or description to the metaphor or simile – the phrase or word which flashes a vivid picture on the inner screen of the mind. Stories or parables can be extremely telling, but they require considerable powers of imagination to invent or adapt, and qualities of voice and timing which are uncommon. Try to invent a new parable like 'The Good Samaritan' or 'The Prodigal Son' and you will see what I mean. Count the number of friends you have who can really tell a joke well, and compare them to those who think they can! Vivid stories and parables are invaluable, but they should be relevant, clear and simple.

Metaphors and similes are essentially comparisons. With metaphors the comparison is introduced neat and sudden; with similes it is signalled in advance by the words 'like...' or 'as...'. They can help in two ways. First, they can aid clarity, because our progress in any field often depends upon our ability to relate the unknown to the known. If we can place the unfamiliar beside the familiar, so that we can explore the 'likes' and 'unlikes' of the comparison, it helps us to understand what the communicator is getting at. For example the prize-winning journalist Robert Heller could work into an *Observer* piece on management technology: 'A great deal of this essential technology is financial: those who feel that finance is seldom sensible should consider Discounted Cash Flow. That supposedly sophisticated technique is based, roughly, on the simple old adage that a pound in the hand is worth two in the bush.'[8]

Thus we must distinguish between intrinsic and ornamental metaphors and similes. Intrinsic metaphors, like sheep-dogs, work for their living; ornamental ones may add a touch of grace or colour, but they are more like poodles. Of course metaphors can be both useful and attractive: when this happens they bring a refreshing life to whatever is said. In the bread-and-butter communications of our daily professional lives I believe that the priority must go to the intrinsic or working metaphors.

It is difficult for us to bring colour and vitality into our daily speech through striking and apt metaphors because we are so conditioned to think of all such words as poetic extravagances or artificial devices. The cure is to remember that all language has its roots in the concrete: scratch almost any word, lift the Latin varnish from it, and you will find a ready-made picture. For example, 'company' (from *cum panis*) meant originally people who 'shared bread' together, while 'salary' signifies the money a Roman soldier received in place of his *salus* or salt ration. Whether we like it or not our language is photographic already, and in applying the principle of Be Vivid we only have to release the picture power which is already gloriously there.

Power is probably the right word, because our metaphors and similes often come kicking and struggling into the world with a life of their own. Language should serve meaning as method should serve content. But both meaning and content are constantly in danger of 'take-over' bids from language and methods, such as visual aids. The test is always the practical one: do people remember the message or do they only chuckle over the illustrative story or the memorable phrase?

Mixed metaphors are to be avoided unless they are announced. For they betray a muddled mind; they break the principles of clarity and simplicity. Secondly, they are witnesses to the metaphor struggling to dominate the message. We can see this by comparing two examples of personification, the first cousin to metaphor. John Bright M.P., speaking on the eve of the Crimean War, made his hearers in the House of Commons sit up with this vivid image: 'The Angel of Death has been abroad throughout the land; you may almost hear the beating of his wings.' Compare that with the mixed metaphor of an excited Irish

86

politician of a later decade who could solemnly warn his fellow members:

> 'Mr Speaker, I smell a rat. I see it floating in the air;
> and if it is not nipped in the bud, it will burst forth into
> a terrible conflagration that will deluge the world.'

Humour can also add vividness to speaking. No one has yet succeeded in defining humour, nor do we understand all the causes of laughter. Yet we all recognize humour when we see or hear it, and our response is all the more pleasing because it is involuntary. We are being temporarily robbed of our composure, and we surrender it instantly and willingly. Besides bringing light relief and vitality to speaking humour also can serve the secondary purpose of attracting and earthing the tension – sometimes electric – which is present in the situation. Laughter enables us to explode the tension within us, and we are grateful to the jester.

Thus a natural humour may help to make a point vividly and defuse a situation at the same time. Countless illustrations of this twofold role of humour in communication could be given. We enjoy them so much that we pay professional comedians to demonstrate this single attribute of the good speaker for our entertainment, but it is better to observe how practical men use their humour. Arthur Ellis, a World Cup football referee now retired, recently recalled one such incident. Having commented on the problems of maintaining discipline he continued:

> I used to love the humour of the Shackletons and the Laws ... real showmen who put extra sparkle into the game.
>
> There are a score of anecdotes I could tell you about Shack but the one that sticks out in my memory came when he was partnering Trevor Ford against Derby County.
>
> Shack drew the defence and pushed a precise pass to the feet of Ford. I reckoned he was fractionally offside and blew up.
>
> As Shack ran past me he shouted for my hearing: 'That was a bloody awful decision, wasn't it, Trevor?'
>
> I smiled to myself and got on with the game. Some time later Shack beat three men in a magnificent run but mis-hit his shot and almost put the ball against a corner flag. 'And that was a bloody awful shot,' I shouted, and we all laughed out loud.[9]

Thus the principle of Be Vivid starts in the heart, in the interest, enthusiasm and commitment which the subject has kindled in the potential communicator. But it has to find expression in arrangement and delivery. Pictures bring vividness, be they actual or verbal. The visual metaphor or simile is a short and vivid picture, which also aids clarity and simplicity. Humour can also enliven working communications, for laughter and boredom cannot live long together. Communication is a serious business, but it need rarely be a solemn one. But the vividness of image or humour should be such as not to draw attention to itself. Far from taking off on an independent life of its own, and becoming 'art for art's sake', it should always serve the *aim* in the centre of the Communication Star.

BE NATURAL

To a large extent the first four principles can be applied before a talk or speech begins, even though there are only a few minutes to consider what you are going to say and how you will put it. The principle of Be Natural, however, belongs primarily to the stage of delivery: it governs our manner of speaking. Of course it can also influence all our preliminary thinking, for both the subject and the methods chosen should be natural to use, or have become so.

When it comes to speaking, art (like all grace) should not destroy nature but perfect it. Here one of the points of the Communication Star – the situation – can be especially troublesome. We all know how difficult it can be to act naturally in certain circumstances. We should think nothing of jumping a four-foot-wide stream, but a similar gap several thousand feet up on a mountain cliff can make us freeze with nerves. The principle of Be Natural invites us to shut off the danger signals from the situation, and speak as naturally as if we were standing before our own hearths. Easier said than done. Yet the art of relaxing can help to fight off the strained voice. The natural and relaxed manners of the experienced television entertainers give us plenty of models for observation.

The principle of naturalness is not, however, a licence to be our own worst selves before a captive audience. Relaxation can so easily slip into sloppiness, just as 'doing what comes naturally' may be sometimes rightly interpreted by the audience as an inconsiderate lack of adequate preparation. Nor should friendly mumbling or inconsequential chatter, laced with 'you knows', be mistaken for naturalness. The principles must be taken together. Speaking distinctly is the principle of Be Clear applied to the actual activity of speaking: it is our ordinary natural speech magnified to meet the larger situation.

Many of the textbooks on communication devote much space to the techniques of breathing, intonation, pronunciation and gesturing. Doubtless there is much to be learnt here, but it is possible to overstress the importance of these elocutionary actions. Beyond the essentials of clear and distinct speech there is little that must be said. Variety in tone and pitch stem from one's natural interest and enthusiasm. If they are 'put on' or practised in front of the mirror, the result can seem self-conscious and even theatrical – in a word, unnatural. For self-training purposes, however, I have included in Appendix 1 a digest of the advice of one specialist on the use of the voice.

Being natural should not be equated entirely with vocal relaxation. It includes giving expression in our speech to the natural emotions that human flesh is heir to. Our education and culture teach us to suppress any public display of emotion, and this can make communication sound stilted and artificial. It is unfashionable for orators to weep in public nowadays, although Churchill brushed the odd tear from his eye on more than one occasion. But naturalness follows if we allow the emotions of the moment – interest, curiosity, anger or passion – to colour our voices and movements. Yet they should serve the voice and not master it. 'I act best when my heart is warm and my head cool', declared the actor Joseph Jefferson, and all who speak might echo his sentiment.

Summary

It would be possible to put forward fifty or more rules for public speaking, with sub-rules to cover the 'set piece' situations and the more 'off the cuff' ones which characterize the working life of managers, supervisors and shop stewards in all kinds of organizations, besides the wider community. But nobody could remember such a list, let alone apply them. It is much better to have before us the five memorable principles. These principles take the values most relevant to communication and put them to work.

BE PREPARED
BE CLEAR
BE SIMPLE
BE VIVID
BE NATURAL

Mere techniques cannot reproduce these principles. The starting point is to recognize their value and importance: not merely for writers or journalists, but for the practical ends of everyday life. Peter Drucker puts it like this:

Managers have to learn to know language, to understand what words are and what they mean. Perhaps most important, they have to acquire a respect for language as man's most precious gift and heritage. The manager must understand the meaning of the old definition of rhetoric as 'the art which draws men's hearts to the love of true knowledge.' Without ability to motivate by means of the written and spoken word or the telling number, a manager cannot be successful.[10]

CHAPTER SIX

BETTER LISTENING

Lord Chief Justice: You hear not what I say to you.
        Falstaff: Very well, my Lord, very well; rather
                an't please you, it is the disease of
                not listening, the malady of not
                marking, that I am troubled withal.
                        SHAKESPEARE, Henry IV

Many of us, like Falstaff, suffer from 'the disease of not listening'. All too often listening is regarded negatively as what you do while you are awaiting your turn to talk. Yet listening is such a positive contribution to the total business of 'commoning', or attaining the common aim, that it deserves our attention in its own right. Thus we must start with a clear distinction between hearing and listening. The first is mundane; the second is rare. To be good listeners means essentially the same as to be good communicants or receivers.

Most books on communication seem to ignore listening altogether. The few which deal with it launch straightaway into 'Do's' and 'Don'ts'. But it is worth pausing to recollect the Communication Star in Chapter Two, which suggests that communication is a result of an inter-action between six points. So far we have been looking at these points through the eyes of a 'sender'; now we shall be considering them from the point of view of someone who wants to receive.

It is natural for us to focus first upon the relation of communicant (in this case, listener) to communicator. As the 'Charge of the Light Brigade' case-study illustrated, the quality of relationship between two people will influence any communications which take place between them. But the lines which link the receiver to the content, the methods employed, and the situation or setting, will also influence the duration and quality of his listening. Moreover the communicant is not merely acted upon; he also exports his own radiations along the lines of the Star to its other 'points' — the speaker, the content and the method or forms of expression. When he is lacking in ability as a listener the star will inevitably lose its lustre. On the other hand, a good listener can help to redress an unbalanced star. And so listening is a vital ingredient in the creative pattern-making of all human communication. Indeed William Pitt went as far as to declare that 'eloquence is in the assembly,

91

not in the speaker.'

Nine Symptoms of Poor Listening

Of course it is possible to find people who do not suffer at all from Falstaff's 'disease of not listening,' but they are uncommon. Most of us, having fought an uncertain war against our self-centredness, succumb to minor bouts of 'not-listening' at any time; some are as permanently incapacitated by it as are the physically deaf to sounds. What can we do about it? The first step is to diagnose one's own case; or, better still, ask an honest husband or wife to help us to do so. You may like to use the following nine symptoms of poor listening as a guide to some self-analysis. Should you score 100 per cent under each heading, being totally void of all the nine failings in the judgement of even your most perceptive and honest critic, then you can safely ignore the rest of this chapter!

1 CONDEMNING THE SUBJECT AS UNINTERESTING WITHOUT A HEARING

'There is no such thing as an uninteresting subject,' wrote G.K. Chesterton, 'there are only uninteresting people.' Sufferers with this symptom disagree with Chesterton: they have defined their own 'interests' and built them like town walls around their lives. You have to storm the gates to get in. The remedy is to realize that condemning any subject as uninteresting is a public acknowledgement of being an uninteresting person. Of course there are shades and grades: we develop our own pattern of interests. But the failure comes when we do not add to the judgement 'uninteresting' the qualifying phrase – 'for me'. If we admit that the universe is so designed that interest impregnates it, then a subject is always potentially interesting – however dull the speaker may be, or however impoverished our own bank balance of interest at the time.

A variation on this symptom is to pre-judge a speaker as uninteresting for some reason or another. 'Can any good come out of Nazareth?' asked the Pharisees. So we condemn large numbers of people to silence, because we do not believe they have an interesting contribution to make. Or because their last efforts have been unconstructive or long-winded. Yet in organizations of all kinds much of the conversation revolves around work, and people's jobs are sources of endless interest. We all have only one piece of the jig-saw of meaning. Other people have always learnt some skills, some insights or some facts which we know not, and thus – strictly speaking – we never meet anyone who has nothing to teach us. Persuading him to give us a free lesson is the art of listening. The more he cares for his work the more he will respond. Plato, one of the world's top ten intellects, loved to listen to seamen, farmers and craftsmen talking about their skills. There is no record that he ever comdemned anyone or anything as incapable of arousing his interest.

2 CRITICISING THE SPEAKER'S DELIVERY OR AIDS

One way of expressing one's non-listening ability is to fasten on the speaker's delivery or the quality of his audio-visual aids. Some trick of pronunciation, an accent or impediment, involuntary movements or mannerisms: all these can be seized upon as excuses for not listening to the meaning. Or the audio-visual aids, which like Hannibal's elephants can be a terror to their own side, can go on rampage and distract a weak listener. It is hard to listen when the delivery is bad and the audio-visual aids out of control, but such occasions do sort out the hearers from the listeners.

3 SELECTIVE LISTENING

Selective listening should not be confused with listening in waves of attention, which is in fact a characteristic of the good listener. Selective listening means that you are programmed to turn a deaf ear to certain topics or themes. Adolf Hitler achieved a unique mastery in this field: he only wanted to hear good news. Those who brought him bad news, or told him the truth, encountered a glassy look and personal insult, if not worse. The danger in selective listening is that it can become habitual and unconscious: we become totally unaware that we only want to listen to certain people or a limited range of ego-boosting news, or that we are filtering and straining information. But our friends and colleagues know full well. And they start pre-digesting the material for us, omitting vital pieces and garnishing the rest with half-truths. And in the corridors they may mutter, 'You can't tell him the truth – he doesn't want to know.'

4 INTERRUPTING

Persistent interrupting is the most obvious badge of the bad listener. Of course interrupting is an inevitable part of everyday conversation, springing from the fact that we can think faster than the other person can talk. So the listener can often accurately guess the end of a sentence or remark. The nuisance interrupter, however, either gets it wrong or else – even worse – he elbows in with a remark which shouts out the fact that he has not been listening to the half-completed capsule of meaning. He may often be working on his own next piece of talk, and therefore be literally too busy to listen. Once the remark is ready, or even half-fitted, he lets it fly and starts winding up for the next one.

5 DAY DREAMING

Day dreaming may be a natural escape from an intolerable situation, but it can also be a symptom of poor listening. It is difficult to think two things at the same time. The day dreamer has 'switched off,' and his attention is given to an inner television screen. Some inner agenda has gained precedence over what is being said to him. The poor listener has a monkey always on his mental shoulder. There is a disconnected chatter going into his left inner ear — that holiday, what Mr Jones said, did I switch my car lights off, if only I was managing director I would ... Emotions can project colour pictures on the inner-screen and turn up the sound. Then — farewell to listening.

6 SUCCUMBING TO EXTERNAL DISTRACTIONS

Uncomfortable chairs, noise, heat or cold, sunlight or gloom: the situation can master the listener and drown the speaker and the content. The good listener will try to deal with the distraction in some helpful way; the poor one allows it to dominate his mind and rob him of attention. The higher the quality of listening the less power externals have over the relationship of communicant and communicator. Listening affirms or builds the relationship in the teeth of forces at work to disintegrate it. The weak listener has no extra reserves to call upon to counter such trying circumstances as falling bombs or cocktail parties.

7 EVADING THE DIFFICULT OR TECHNICAL

Such is our addiction to the clear, simple and vivid that none of us cares for the difficult, long and dull presentation, and we throw the sponge in too soon. We have a low tolerance for anything which even threatens to be difficult, coupled with an impatience at the inability of the speaker to save our time and energy by applying the principles of good speaking. But what is at issue is not merely his ability as a speaker but our skill as listeners. If the path has to be tortuous and uphill, the stout-hearted listener will follow. The lazy listener gives up at the first obstacle.

8 SUBMITTING TO EMOTIONAL WORDS

A symptom of the poor listener is his vulnerability to trigger words. Words enter the atmosphere carrying certain associations, pleasant or unpleasant. An unskilled speaker can trigger off a minefield in the minds of an audience, and yet be as innocent as a child out at play. Our minds are like a convoy in this respect, and the poor listener gives in at the first mine explosions! At once thought stops, and his ready-made responses come into play. The man or the topic is instantly categorized; emotions rise and throw us out of tune with the speaker. Once lost, that harmony of relationship, the essential partnership, is not easily restored.

9 GOING TO SLEEP

Or the Mad Hatter Syndrome. When indulged in frequently, nodding off to sleep can be a symptom of a poor listener. For the art of listening requires a background of sufficient sleep, a fact which the poor practitioner habitually ignores. His late nights and impressive tiredness may be signs that he has not understood the importance of listening. Tiredness does affect our listening. The tactical remedy lies in that neglected commodity, will-power; the strategic answer is to insist upon enough sleep. The poor listener is chronically short of both.

Towards Better Listening

Awareness that in varying degrees we are all victims of poor listening habits is a necessary if painful start to a programme of self-help in this area of communication. But once the 'disease of not listening' has been diagnosed we may have to do more than treat the symptoms, for the root of the malady sometimes lies deep inside us, in basic attitudes to life, other people and ourselves. No form of management training and perhaps no kind of medicine, can reach down into those depths and change us entirely. We can split the atom, but we do not know a technique for transforming the nucleus of self-centredness into other-centredness. Yet most of us are not such hopeless cases, and beneath our superficial pre-occupation with self there lies a ready and willing spirit waiting to share in the experience and life of others. It is more a question of projecting ourselves into orbit.

In order to escape the forces of gravity which pull us back to our own centre we can be helped by some common-sense guides. Ten of these are listed and discussed briefly later in this chapter. But first we must consider again the importance of planning and preparation for creating the essential background to good listening.

Being Prepared to Listen

'A busy man', the saying goes, 'finds time for everything.' Somehow the 'still life' picture of a person intent on listening does not seem to fit in with the contemporary image of the business man as Busy Man. Like the White Rabbit in *Alice in Wonderland* the latter always seems to be 'late for a very important date'. Frenetic activity, telephones ringing, secretaries hovering, typewriters clattering: these are so-called realities. All these externals can provide most respectable excuses for becoming poor listeners. 'So sorry – I should *like* to have listened to you, but I just do not have time...'

The answer, of course, is to make the time. To have the necessary leisure to listen attentively and not merely hear what is said requires a well-kept life. The application of the principle of making time might begin with ruthless examination of where one's time goes, and a total or partial reorganization of the working day. It is difficult to listen unless you have with you the right person, at the right time and in the right place. Consequently this first principle is not a mere exhortation: it is an invitation to consider priorities against purpose, aims and objectives.

In her book *Managers and Their Jobs* (1967) Dr Rosemary Stewart has presented the evidence from 160 managers which confirms the need to plan one's time if the necessary conditions for listening are to be created:

A manager may be able to save more time by organizing his discussions with other people efficiently than in any other way. The research findings underlined the truth of the statement that managers work with other people. The average amount of time that the 160 managers spent with other people was 66 per cent. Is this a high proportion of the working day well spent? To answer this ... the manager must know who are the people he should be seeing and how much time he should normally spend with them. He should know to whom he should be available, and when. He and his secretary should know who ought to have immediate access to him.

When a manager has a visitor his secretary should know in what circumstances he is to be interrupted, but should otherwise ensure that the conversation is undisturbed. His visitor should never need to resort to the strategy reportedly adopted by Keynes in a visit to Roosevelt. The story, which may be apocryphal, is that Keynes paid a visit to Roosevelt, which was interrupted by frequent telephone calls. After some time Keynes left the room and telephoned Roosevelt, who expressed surprise. Keynes replied, 'I realize that the telephone is the only way to get your attention.[1]

Through good planning and diary control it is possible to lessen the frittering away of one's own time, and — what may be worse — to keep the interruption of other people's time down to the essential minimum. We have no more precious gift to offer another person than our time, and the art lies in spending it both carefully and generously.

Sometimes, however, the programme goes wrong or events crowd in upon one. The 'set-piece' interviews and meetings, with their times thoughtfully budgeted, do make better listening possible, but what about the less structured and less predictable parts of a busy person's life? Here the answer is to create opportunities in the midst of the hustle and bustle, to make time and space just as a great footballer can find that fraction of a second to turn on the ball and score where many lesser players just cannot react fast enough. In other words, the principle of making time can apply to minutes and seconds as well as hours or mornings. Sometimes it is possible to clear a minute or five minutes to listen, which will be worth half-an-hour or more of fitful interrupted hearing to the person concerned.

In these moments, which we create out of nothing, the rank or importance of the person should count not at all. What is vital is that the person wants to say something which matters to him and concerns us, however indirectly. If one cannot guarantee to listen immediately it is always possible to fix an appointment when one can. It takes a well-kept life to be free to listen in the cracks and crevasses of a full timetable, but it can be done. For without making some time totally available there can be no listening.

Preparations may be compared to ploughing up the ground in order to make it more receptive. Background knowledge about the subject and the speaker can aid listening. More often than not one's preparations must be general rather than particular, but sometimes it is possible to do some preliminary reading or discussing which helps one to select what will be the areas meriting special attention in the forthcoming meeting.

Adequate sleep and general fitness may also contribute to the production of attention. Listening, if properly done, can be physically demanding. 'Efficient listening is characterized by a quick action of the heart, a fast circulation of blood, and a small rise in body temperature. It is energy-burning and energy-consuming. It is dynamic and constructive. Therefore, if you would listen well, you have to expend some energy in the process.'[2] Planning and control of the written or unwritten timetable, preliminary preparations and physical freshness:

under such treatments the 'disease of not listening' must begin to respond.

Thus, like any game or battle, the outcome of a meeting as far as the communication goes is largely determined before play or action begins. As we have seen, this is as true for the listening part of the equation as it is for the speaking role. And, of course, we usually play both parts in alternation. Thus a good listener is made in solitude, in times of reflection and thought far removed from the dust and heat of conversation.

The clearest evidence of his existence is the shape of his diary, by the careful but generous use of his time and the flexible control he maintains over interviews or meetings. Also his mind is well-kept: skeletons are not rattling in the cupboards of his mind. Internal and external distractions can be often foreseen and dealt with, but there are times when we just have to brace ourselves and deliberately compartmentalize our minds. The seas may be flooding the fo'c'sle but we have to slam and screw a hatch, and turn with our back to it in order to listen. As the actors say, 'the show must go on.'

Ten Guides to Good Listening

Based on a study of the 100 best and the 100 worst listeners in a freshman class at the University of Minnesota, Ralph G. Nicholas has produced ten useful guides to listening. [3] Although I have retained his headings and most of his comments (given in quotes) I have added some of my own. They can be described briefly, as most of them are positive versions of the negative symptoms of poor listening.

1 FIND AREA OF INTEREST

From the discussion above it can be seen that this is almost the golden rule of good listening. It is a rare subject which does not have any possible interest or use for us, our friends or families. We naturally screen what is being said for its interest or value.

2 JUDGE CONTENT, NOT DELIVERY

'Many listeners alibi inattention to a speaker by thinking to themselves: "Who would listen to such a character? What an awful voice! Will he ever stop reading from his notes?" The good listener moves on to a different conclusion, thinking, "But wait a minute... I'm not interested in his personality or delivery. I want to find out what he knows. Does this man know some things that I need to know?"'

3 HOLD YOUR FIRE

'Overstimulation is almost as bad as understimulation and the two together constitute the twin evils of inefficient listening. The over-stimulated listener gets too excited, or excited too soon, by the speaker. The aroused person usually becomes preoccupied by trying to do three things simultaneously: calculate what hurt is being done to his own pet ideas; plot an embarrassing question to ask the speaker; enjoy all the discomfiture visualized for the speaker once the devastating reply to him is launched. With these things going on subsequent passages go unheard.'

4 LISTEN FOR IDEAS

The good listener focuses on the main ideas. He does not fasten on to the peripheral themes or seize on some fact or other, which may block his mind from considering the central ideas.

5 BE FLEXIBLE

There is no one system for making notes. The good listener may employ four or five methods, depending on the other factors in the Communication Star, such as the content and situation.

6 WORK AT LISTENING

Good listening takes energy. Attention is a form of directed energy. 'We ought to establish eye contact and maintain it; to indicate by posture and facial expression that the occasion and the speaker's effort are a matter of real concern to us. When we do these things we help the speaker to express himself more clearly, and we in turn profit by better understanding the improved communication we have helped him to achieve.'

In his role, silence can be as expressive of the listener's personality as words are for the speaker. If a sculpture is a work of art compounded of materials and space, so communication is made up from words *and* silence. Silence is not a negative vacuum; it can convey warm and positive feelings which can help or hinder the communicator. The best silence, corrected and deepened by asking the right questions, is an influence felt by the other person, willing him to give of his best.

7 RESIST DISTRACTIONS

'A good listener instinctively fights distraction. Sometimes the fight is easily won — by closing a door, shutting off a radio, moving closer to the person talking, or asking him to speak louder. If the distractions cannot be met that easily, then it becomes a matter of concentration.'

8 EXERCISE YOUR MIND
Good listeners regard apparently difficult or demanding presentations or speakers as challenges to their mental abilities.

9 KEEP YOUR MIND OPEN
Effective listeners try to identify their own prejudices, blind spots and semiconscious assumptions. Instead of turning a deaf ear, they seek to improve upon their perception and understanding precisely in those areas.

10 CAPITALIZE ON THOUGHT SPEED
'Most persons talk at a speed of 125 words per minute. There is good evidence that if thought were measured in words per minute, most of us could think easily at about four times that rate.

'The good listener uses his thought speed to advantage; he constantly applies his spare thinking time to what is being said. It is not difficult once one has a definite pattern of thought to follow. To develop such a pattern we should:

- 'Try to anticipate what a person is going to say.
- Mentally summarize what the person has been saying. What point has he made already, if any?
- Weigh the speaker's evidence by mentally questioning it. Ask yourself, "Am I getting the full picture, or is he telling me only what will prove his point?"
- Listen between the lines. The speaker doesn't always put everything that's important into words. The changing tones and volume of his voice may have a meaning. So may his facial expressions, the gestures he makes with his hands, the movement of his body.

Not capitalizing on thought speed is our greatest single handicap. Yet, through listening training, this same differential can readily be converted into our greatest asset.'

The Ethics of Listening
Cato's definition of an orator — 'a good man skilled in speaking' — can also be adapted and applied to listeners. There are indeed skills in listening, but it would be a mistake to reduce good listening to a matter of techniques. Professional listeners — priests, doctors and journalists —

100

are bound by their own codes of ethics. But the natural activity of listening itself may possess its own intrinsic morality. The good listener, for example, is one who can be trusted to keep a confidence, or to use what he hears only to the advantage of the speaker. Certainly we feel betrayed if someone has misrepresented us, broken a confidence or in any way diminished the poles of trust which must support the slender line of communication. Integrity is as essential for the good listener as it is for the communicator.

Conclusion

A person's listening will express his attitude to other people as surely as the way in which he speaks to them. Indeed, writes Robert T. Oliver, 'for the real master of communication... listening and talking are interwoven... like the warp and weft of a piece of cloth. When he is listening, he is standing at the threshold of his companion's mind; and when he is talking, he invites his auditor to stand at the doorway of his own thought.'[4] To be able to move easily and flexibly from one position to the other in pursuit of a common subject or theme, such is good communication.

Above all listening should be a positive influence which enables or supports the speaker in the difficult business of transferring thought, with all its shades of meaning, into the coinage of sentences and words. Silence can be made to express positive and warm encouragement, or it can lamely convey negative feelings or indifference. Silence and attention form the basis of listening, but the mind is not a blank page or empty barrel. Listening is only valuable because it creates the necessary conditions in which the mind can get to work to sort out, restructure and digest what is being said. Lastly, it could be added that attentive silence should bear in it the seed of willingness to make an appropriate response, be it action, understanding or unity. 'The effective listener', concludes Dominick Barbara, 'is one who *uses* silence as he uses talk — with an eager, alive and generous desire to share.'[5]

CHAPTER SEVEN

CLEAR WRITING

For a man to write well, there are required three
necessaries — to read the best authors, observe
the best speakers, and much exercise in his own style.

BEN JONSON

Ben Jonson's words remind us that there are no sharp divisions between the different modes of communication: our competence with the written word depends to some degree upon our abilities as speakers, listeners or readers. Certainly managers or leaders in all fields have plenty of occasions for 'much exercise' in writing: letters, memoranda, reports, minutes and notes abound. Research confirms the common-sense observation, as Dr. Rosemary Stewart's survey of 160 managers has witnessed:

> Managers varied enormously in the amount of time they spent on writing, dictating, reading, and figurework. The average was 36 per cent of total working time, with a range from 7 to 84 per cent. The average is made up of 26 per cent spent on writing, dictating, and reading company material, 8 per cent on figurework — though in some jobs it may have been difficult to separate figurework from writing — and 2 per cent on reading external material for work purposes.[1]

In terms of the Communication Star, such devices as books, reports, letters etc. are *methods* for conveying a content from communicators to communicants. The situation or context in which the paper will be read cannot always be known or predicted. Nor can the writer watch the face of the reader, and adjust his message and delivery in the light of his reactions. Thus it is possible to become extremely suspicious about the usefulness of the written word. 'Paper does not communicate', as one manager bluntly declared to me once.

On the other hand writing it down does have some obvious advantages. The written word is at least potentially permanent. The reader can refer back to it and ponder the meaning. Moreover, especially through the medium of print in all its forms — from typewriter to printing press – the written word can convey meaning to those widely separated in distance from the writer, and in a more readily accessible way than – for instance – the recorded spoken word. Lastly, whether we like it or not, writing is here to stay for the foreseeable future as an essential ingredient in working and personal life.

The Importance of Style

Writing is obviously made up of words, phrases and sentences. There are certain rules and conventions over such matters as punctuation, spelling and arrangement. Many or all of these we learn in elementary and secondary education, or teach ourselves later on. But the combinations of parts are so varied that we each develop a method of writing which can be as distinctive as our finger-prints. Our writing computer gets programmed with certain favourite words, phrases or constructions, which trigger off certain other lines of language when they appear on the blank sheet before us. For this manner of expression, characteristic of a particular writer, we can best use the word *style*, borrowed from *stylus*, the name of the Latin tool for incising letters on wax tablets.

Style bears two main meanings. It can stand first for an individual's unique mode of expression, and secondly for the general mode which distinguishes some class of writers or writings. A discussion of the first belongs properly to the art of literary writing, but we should be wary here as elsewhere of making a false dichotomy. Although the aim of business writing (in any sphere) is to get a message over (and not 'to express oneself'), it is important to be aware that – again like it or not – our style will communicate to the reader something about ourselves as persons. An ill-chosen word can jar like a wrong note; a sloppy sentence can suggest muddled or woolly thinking. 'Reading between the lines' is an unavoidably human activity. 'Use what language you will,' wrote Emerson, 'you can never say anything but what you are.'

Thus the first priority of the working writer is to concentrate on the general characteristics – or style – needed for business writing. Only secondly should he study some of the literary 'tricks of the trade' and then only to avoid accidentally conveying the wrong message about himself to the reader. Yet that does not mean that his writing should be totally devoid of grace. Pleasure boats or gilded yachts were no rivals in beauty to sail clippers. Yet those tall ships carried cases of tea or bales of cotton stacked within their holds. Working books, reports or letters must also carry cargo, but they too can do it with elegance.

In one important respect the stylistic demand is more severe for the manager than the literary writer. The manager is dealing more explicitly in the commodities of money and time. Long letters or memos cost money in terms of secretarial wages and postal charges. Thus conciseness is an essential for the business writer. Not for him the luxury of spreading himself over many pages. Of course the professional writer should also wage war on unnecessary length, although his definition of 'necessary' may include a larger place for self-expression through the tricks and skills of his trade. For he is being paid to delight as well as to instruct and move his readers. But both manager and author are drawing upon the precious limited time of the reader, those minutes and hours which measure out our lives. Wasting time is wasting life. Thus, above all, the manager has to aim at an accurate brevity, or (as Herbert Spencer said) at the 'economy of the reader's or hearer's attention'.

The Prose Revolution

The Prose Revolution, like the Industrial Revolution, owes much to the impact of science on life. As early as the seventeenth century the first historian of the Royal Society, Thomas Spratt, mentioned their rejection of the 'amplications, digressions and swellings of style' in contemporary writers in favour of a 'close, natural and naked way of speaking'. But the preference for such a style has its roots deep in history. The Prose Revolution, as we may call its triumph into an orthodoxy, in this century, was fed by many underground streams.

As in the case of science the Revolution was founded upon a search for immutable laws which could yield a list of 'Do's and Don'ts' guaranteeing an effective and pleasing style for the busy writer. In 1906 H.W. and F.G. Fowler opened the first chapter of *The King's English* with this salvo:

> Any one who wishes to become a good writer should endeavour, before he allows himself to be tempted by the more showy qualities, to be direct, simple, brief, vigorous, and lucid. This general principle may be translated into practical rules in the domain of vocabulary as follows:-
>
> Prefer the familiar word to the far-fetched.
> Prefer the concrete word to the abstract.
> Prefer the single word to the circumlocution.
> Prefer the short word to the long.
> Prefer the Saxon word to the Romance (i.e. Latin)

These rules are given roughly in order of merit; the last is also the least.

Another influential writer, Sir Arthur Quiller-Couch, in his Cambridge lecture 'On the Art of Writing' published in 1916, added one more rule:

> Generally use transitive verbs, that strike their object; and use them in the active voice, eschewing the stationary passive, with its little auxiliary is's and was's, and its participles getting into the light of your adjectives, which should be few. For, as a rough law, by his use of the straight verb and by his economy of adjectives you can tell a man's style, if it be masculine or neuter, writing or 'composition'.

At the invitation of the Treasury in 1948 Sir Ernest Gowers produced his paperback *Plain Words*, a guide to the use of English by civil servants. Gowers, in common with Quiller-Couch, suspected pedantry in the last two rules proposed by the Fowler brothers, but he was equally critical of Quiller-Couch's substitutes. Instead he suggested that the essence of both the sets of advice could be summed up in three rules:

> Use no more words than are necessary to express your meaning, for if you use more you are likely to obscure it and to tire your reader. In particular do not use superfluous adjectives and adverbs and do not use roundabout phrases where single words would serve.
>
> Use familiar words rather than the far-fetched, for the familiar are more likely to be readily understood.
>
> Use words with a precise meaning rather than those that are vague, for they will obviously serve better to make your meaning clear; and in particular prefer concrete words to abstract, for they are more likely to have a precise meaning:

Meanwhile Rudolf Flesch had translated and popularized Fowler and Quiller-Couch for American readers in a series of books, beginning with *The Art of Plain Talk* in 1946. His message had a marked effect, for American 'businessese' was ripe for the sickle as Whitehall 'officialese' had been. Flesch condensed his advice into no less than twenty-five rules:

> Write about people, things, and facts.
> Write as you talk.
> Use contractions.
> Use the first person.
> Quote what was said.

Quote what was written.
Put yourself in the reader's place.
Don't hurt the reader's feelings.
Forestall misunderstandings.
Don't be too brief.
Plan a beginning, middle, and end.
Go from the rule to the exception, from the familiar to the new.
Use short names and abbreviations.
Use pronouns rather than repeating nouns.
Use verbs rather than nouns.
Use the active voice and a personal subject.
Use small, round figures.
Specify. Use illustrations, cases, examples.
Start a new sentence for each new idea.
Keep your sentences short.
Keep your paragraphs short.
Use direct questions.
Underline for emphasis.
Use parentheses for casual mention.
Make your writing interesting to look at.

To measure progress in the Anglo-American war on verbiage Flesch and others developed some quantifiable methods of estimating readability by counting up certain kinds of words in limited samples and calculating a score which was then checked against a scale. But readability is not the same as comprehensibility. Whether or not people understand does not depend primarily on the choice of root words, but on the quality of thought behind the language. The quantifying techniques 'will certainly not stop a bad writer from producing an illogically constructed text.'[2]

The less happy results in the 'prose-engineering movement' comes from the human tendency to treat as literal rules what should really be regarded as principles. We need to be able to break down abstract principles into more concrete rules, but the impulse in many people is then to forget the principles and fasten exclusively on the rules, holding them to be 100% applicable in all cases. But this policy soon lands a writer on the rocks. A rule such as 'Prefer the short word to the long', for example, if taken too far ignores the fact that sometimes the long word is the right word. Thus the superficial application of the Flesch formulas could result in a deliberate 'talking down' (or 'writing down') to a supposed level of intelligence and vocabulary in the reader. The outcome in America, according to *Fortune* magazine, has been a kind of managerial pidgin English or an inverted form of gobbledygook. In other words a new orthodoxy, full of autocratic rights and wrongs, has begun to emerge.

Rules do have their place, but they ought to be concrete expressions of principles and not substitutes for them. One cannot make lasting improvements in style by manipulating language in a superficial way. The principles have to govern how the mind works, or what it seeks. Take simplicity as an example. Most of Flesch's rules seem to guarantee the golden egg of simplicity. But slavishly followed do they not end up by producing only broiler chickens capable of *simpliste* writing or talking? As the *Fortune* article on 'The Language of Business' perceptively comments:

> Simplicity is an elusive, almost complex thing. It comes from discipline and organization of thought, intellectual courage – and many other attributes more hard won than by short words and short sentences. For plain talk – honest plain talk – is the reward of simplicity, not the means to it. The distinction may seem slight, but it is tremendously important. [3]

Thus we are led back to the principles which should govern both speaking and writing. Be Prepared, Be Clear, Be Simple, Be Vivid and Be Natural. These should not be seen as separate or detachable guides or rules: they ought to qualify each other like checks and balances in any situation, and it is the complex of all five that matters. Be Prepared, for example, ought to include a knowledge of the way other men have written effectively, distilled into such rules as 'prefer the active to the passive verb', as well as the accepted customs over spelling and punctuation. But this should be balanced by the principle Be Natural. The best writers, like the naturally good soldiers of ancient days, are those who have undergone the formal drills and manoeuvres of their discipline, and then been allowed to revert to their former ferocious selves.

As another example, the need for simplicity in language must be balanced against the first principle, which is clarity. All communication, like sketching or painting, involves leaving some things out. The substance and aids to accuracy – stating all the relevant facts, defining terms, following logical steps – demand that certain things should be kept in, even at the expense of brevity. Over-brief or mutilated writing inevitably creates the need for further correcting communications, and so nothing is gained.

In the case of writing we should have swallowed the drill book of grammar (or usage), punctuation, spelling, idiom and composition during our schooldays. The problem, of course, is that we do not have anything much to write about then, and so it can all seem a rather pointless exercise. Only later, when we try to say what is important, or vital, and when the octopus of gobbledygook wraps its long arms around us, do we wish that we had paid more attention to those Ancient Mariners, our teachers. Many textbooks on business communication seek to remedy this deficiency with chapters on such topics as punctuation, spelling and syntax. But these should have been mastered at school. Fortunately there are plenty of good cheap books which can either remedy early deficiencies in our education or provide 'refresher courses' in the more detailed customs of idiom and punctuation. But the spirit matters more than the letter. 'The formal rules of grammar can be taught,' wrote G. H. Vallins, 'but not the indefinable spirit that underlies usage.'[4]

When actually writing it is difficult to remember all these rules and regulations anyway. With plenty of practice and friendly critics the rules governing the selection of words should have become as habitual as the proverbial 'dotting of i's and crossing of t's'. Certainly in practice we do need such rules as those proposed by Fowler, Flesch, Quiller-Couch and others, for they form the bridge in writing between the more abstract principles and the tangible bricks-and-mortar of nouns and verbs. They provide techniques for injecting mental clarity, simplicity and vitality into the medium of the written word.

Word Power

The principle of preparation implies an expanding vocabulary. Many of the rules advocated choices of words from many possibilities, e.g. 'prefer the concrete word to the abstract.' Obviously such rules imply a certain vocabulary. But there is a dilemma over selecting the 'right' word. The 500 most common words, according to *Webster's Dictionary*, have some 14,000 meanings between them. Thus if you use any one of them it may be necessary to hedge it with definitions or qualification. On the other hand the rarer but more accurate word may be unintelligible to the other person without translation. Most people in the United Kingdom use around 8,000 words. But they can understand many more than they use. Thus the writer is not limited to the colloquial language, even though he must eschew the obscure word that will leave his reader in ignorance or waste his time looking it up in the dictionary.

The writer must master the words that are within reach of the reader although they are never on his lips. Cultures and societies, trades and professions, tend to stretch the language, with their own labour-saving words. The Bedouins, for example, have over 300 words for camel; the Eskimo have 23 names for snow but only one word for flower. Our English ancestors produced a wide vocabulary for horses – yet how many city-dwellers today could accurately define a hackney, roan, gelding or pie-bald? Still, we have evolved 220 variants for 'said', and no less than 11,000 words to describe human personality traits.

Television, radio, newspapers, books stamped in the public libraries: all these conspire to maintain the latent vocabulary of the reader. Both the nation's and the individual's vocabularies are rather like stopping commuter trains, with new words getting in and old words alighting at each station. This process is a natural one, but the business writer has to be aware of it. These fashionable newcomers are rarely useful for him, because they are so often already on the way to becoming clichés, smart-sounding words which mean little. The valuable words, those which will keep you company to the end of the journey, are those which you recruit yourself because you like them: they prove useful, intelligible and full of life. The writer has to collect words like other men collect stamps. He also needs to compile his own Rogue's Gallery of words and phrases he does not want to meet, even on a dark night. Yet the final verdict lies with the language as a whole. The words, *mob*, *sham*, *banter*, *bully* and *bamboozle* did not please Dean Swift, nor did Dr Johnson care for *clever*, which he called a 'low word'. But the victory of all these words has been almost complete. We need to fight our own rear-guard actions, but we have to avoid the danger of pedantry, of losing touch with genuine mutations in the language. As the first Queen Elizabeth's tutor Roger Ascham put it:

> He that will write well in any tongue, must follow this counsel of Aristotle, to speak as the common people do, to think as wise men do; and so should every man understand him, and the judgement of wise men allow him.[5]

New Phrases for Old

Few of us have the time or originality to coin new phrases. Thus the advice to avoid the ready-made phrase is pointless. Rather we should shop for them like discriminating housewives. Clichés are phrases that were once striking metaphors or figures of speech which have become so worn with constant use that their face value has diminished. Sometimes, however, such as in our griefs or joys, when we least feel like searching for words, truth can flood back into these dry seaweeds of language. The words we speak to the bereaved may *sound* like clichés, but if sincere they are charged with truth and meaning. Sometimes language must go into mourning. At other more joyful times we have better things to do than to mint new phrases.

For these reasons one should never shut one's mind to someone who writes in clichés. But their reduced capacity as bearers of meaning makes them suspect in most situations. Repetition is subject to the law of diminishing returns. Thus, the principle of Be Vivid is not an invitation to showing off; it should be the prompter of a refreshing variety in phrases. The really dangerous clichés are those which you harbour and use repeatedly without thinking about them.

The language also contains a whole range of readymade adverbial phrases which do take up space without conveying very much, such as 'by and large', 'on the whole', or 'all things being equal'. These have come under much fire during the Prose Revolution, perhaps rather unjustly. For writing should echo our conversation, and most of us do use such everyday phrases. It seems rather purist to insist on their deletion in favour of a single word, like chopping down some endearing and harmless hedges. One can be too neat, as the poet and critic Geoffrey Grigson has observed:

> In a sense I find it easier to write as I grow older. I'm less mystified by what I'm doing. I have more verbal resources and I manage to avoid my own clichés as well as everyone else's. Finding the proper form isn't just a matter of mathematical proportions. I used to write poems which were rather slick — neatly finished off and full of internal rhymes. But now I seem able to avoid that ultra-neatness, as well as the sloppiness that lies in the other direction. There's no longer any feeling of strain, and I suspect it's because I know more surely what it is I want to say.[6]

Tone in Business Letters

The physical conventions for setting out a business letter need not detain us, nor the common-sense importance for deploying a style that is lucid and clear, so that the reader is left in no doubt as to your meaning. But the demand for economy, which I have stressed, can lead to a charge of terseness. It is vital that the *tone* of the letter should reflect your true feelings. The *Oxford English Dictionary* defines *tone* as 'a particular quality, pitch, modulation, or inflexion of the voice expressing... affirmation, interrogation, hesitation, decision, or some feeling or emotion.' Business letters are more likely to be effective if they are written in a tone of courtesy.

Thus courtesy is not an 'optional extra' of good style; it belongs to its very heart. For good style shows that you are at least taking the reader's interest seriously. Quiller-Couch made this point himself in *The Art of Writing*:

> Essentially style resembles good manners. It comes of endeavouring to understand others, of thinking for them rather than yourself — of thinking, that is, with the heart as well as the head... So (says Fénelon) ... 'your words will be fewer and more effectual, and while you make less ado, what you do will be more profitable'.[7]

But what is good manners, as opposed to formal politeness? 'Courtesy results from a balance between *cordiality* and *tact*; *cordiality* being the warmth and friendliness you show toward your reader, *tact* the sensitivity and discretion you show', wrote W. W. Wells in *Communication in Business*[8]. He offered an ominous list of 'Courtesy blunders':

CURTNESS   The flaw which results from inordinate brevity and implies unconcern for your reader.

SARCASM   Most people dislike being on the receiving end of this special form of wit, which is ridiculing by saying the opposite to what you mean.

PEEVISHNESS   Includes such whining remarks as 'You ought to know better.'

ANGER   The roar of anger usually provokes an answering roar, even if it is under your breath.

SUSPICION   Often takes the form of being suspicious about motives.

INSULT   Intentional insults are rare, but unintentional ones are not uncommon — especially in replies to applications for jobs.

ACCUSATION   It is obviously difficult to point an accusing finger and maintain courtesy.

TALKING DOWN	'In an establishment as large as ours, Miss Smith...' The didactic or instructional tone grates in letters, and any teaching has to be done with a light touch.
OVER FAMILIARITY	Cultural differences abound here, e.g. over the use of first names.
PRESUMP-TUOUSNESS	Anyone might be offended by a letter which assumes that he will do something before he has made up his mind to do it. The line between confidence and presumption is a fine one.

Writing business letters implies the desire to do business. One of the tests of a successful business transaction is whether or not the parties are willing to do business with each other again. Lack of courtesy, as exhibited in any or all of the ten symptoms listed above, will diminish this mutual desire to do business or fail to create it in the first place. Thus courtesy has a solid practical and business rationale. But it can also be used to express the 'house style' or ethos of the company and the individual manager. The writer should be able to echo Shakespeare's words in *Timon of Athens*: 'No levell'd malice infects one comma in the course I hold.'[9]

In personal letters especially the note of sincerity is vital. The word means literally a clean or pure sound, and it is an obvious cousin to clarity. Deception, pretence and dishonesty are the opposites to sincerity. Symptoms such as over-humility, obvious flattery, exaggeration and effusiveness betray the presence of insincerity. There are no verbal signs of sincerity: it exists in the writer's mind or not at all. The flavour of the genuine is there or not, according to your palate.

Therefore courtesy, sincerity and a positive firmness make up the tone of the best working correspondence. Examples quoted in this book of such a distinctive tone are the letters of Abraham Lincoln later in this chapter.

In his book *Communication in Business* (1968) W. W. Wells has graphically summed up the ingredients which go into the making of an effective letter (see diagram opposite).

Writing Reports

Few executives in any kind of organization evade writing reports. We cannot do without them. In essence a report is a formal statement of

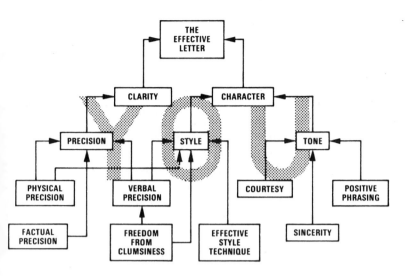

the results of an investigation, or any matter on which definite information is required, made by some person or body who is instructed or asked to do so. The outcome of a report will depend upon a variety of factors in all points of the Communication Star: the intellectual skills of the communicator, the responsiveness of the communicants, the intrinsic merits of the contents, the situation at the time, and the use made of the report method. It is with the last factor we are concerned here.

The first step is to establish whether the report must stand alone or serve in a supporting role to oral communication of some kind — a talk, lecture or a briefing. The latter might take the form of the presentation of a draft report to a small committee, followed by another meeting some time later, when the outline and modifications are explained. The report then acts more as an aide-mémoire. If the situation allows it, some such combination of oral communication and report is much to be preferred, especially if some action is envisaged as a key result.

The principles of clarity and simplicity should be applied in a common-sense way to the structure of the report. It should begin with an introduction, which sets out the essential background and crystallizes the aim and objectives of the report. The latter will have been already foreshadowed by the title. The format, like a book in miniature, should include the name of the author and the date of

113

compilation. The middle body of evidence, information, issues and discussions should be clearly and succinctly arranged in a simple order, sign-posted by chapters, major and minor side headings and numbered paragraphs. The concluding section must leave the reader in no doubt as to the writer's conclusions and recommendations.

The writer's key assumptions should be made manifest at the appropriate places; difficult or technical terms should always be defined. Illustrations, sharing the characteristics of a speaker's good visual aids, can save time and space in the main text, but complicated supporting data should appear as appendices at the end. The minimum requirements for style are not different from those needed for letters or any other forms of business writing. Above all, the report should achieve its stated objective with economy of words, especially where the written word is to be used in alliance with speech.

A checklist of the more detailed questions worth asking when a draft report has been completed is given in Appendix 2. But these are secondary matters. What is essential is the quality of thinking reflected in the report, and the writing ability to arrange and convey it lucidly and concisely to the reader in the right proportion to the spoken word. A victim of many a Whitehall report bulging with undigested evidence, Winston Churchill took the offensive on 9 August 1940 with a famous circular to all Government departments, entitled 'Brevity':

> To do our work we all have to read a mass of papers. Nearly all of them are far too long. This wastes time, while energy has to be spent in looking for essential points.
>
> I ask my colleagues and their staff to see that their reports are shorter.
>
> 1. The aim should be reports which set out the main points in a series of short, crisp paragraphs.
>
> 2. If a report relies on detailed analysis of some complicated factors or on statistics, these should be set out in an appendix.
>
> 3. Often the occasion is best met by submitting not a full report, but a reminder consisting of headings only, which can be expounded orally if needed.
>
> 4. Let us have an end to such phrases as these: 'it is also important to bear in mind the following considerations... or consideration

should be given to the possibility of carrying into effect...' Most
of these woolly phrases are mere padding, which can be left out
altogether, or replaced by a single word. Let us not shrink from
using the short expressive phrase, even if it is conversational.

Reports drawn up on the lines I propose may at first seem rough as
compared with the flat surface of officialese jargon, but the saving in
time will be great, while the discipline of setting out the real points
concisely will prove an aid to clearer thinking.

Winston Churchill may have enjoyed an unfair advantage over his
civil servants in that he had worked for many years as an author and
journalist. Both as writer and orator he had indeed immersed himself
exuberantly in the English language as in a tin bath. But the clarity and
felicity of his letters and memoranda published later in *The Second
World War* issued from a long struggle with the resistances of language
to thought, just as the famous Churchillian voice bore the marks of a
victory over a childhood speech slur.

For the manager who has grasped the need to be aware of the whole
Communication Star and the five principles of speaking, the writing of
a report should present few difficulties. Of course Churchill's demand
for brevity makes for harder work and greater skill. The long-winded
and complicated report takes far less effort. Easy reading makes hard
writing. Moreover false marketing doctrine may persuade us that a thick
sheaf of paper, pompous prose and unintelligible diagrams may
somehow advertise the importance of the subject and the weight of the
conclusions. In fact Albert Sloan's report on General Motors — perhaps
the most influential management report ever written — was not a
lengthy or superficially impressive document. The effectiveness of his
report lay in the accurate location of the issues raised by organizational
size and the practical solutions he proposed. With economy of words
the report conveyed the clear thought of the writer, and he had ample
opportunity to expand it in discussion. Such are the hallmarks of a
good report.

Conclusion

Letters and reports do not exhaust the opportunities for writing well in
professional life. Articles, pamphlets, books: a versatile manager may
tackle them all in the course of his career. In so doing he will evolve his
own methods of work. But any of these forms will be filled by his style,
which may become as distinctive as his signature. While aware that he is

no Michelangelo, a stonemason can still have a craftsman's pride in his handiwork; so can a business writer. He may first have to overcome an ingrained belief that he cannot communicate well on paper, and that there is some art mystique inherent in forging a good style. A training course may give such a person more confidence than reading this book. But it may help him or her to recall Matthew Arnold's encouraging remark: 'People think that I can teach them style. What stuff it all is. Have something to say and say it as clearly as you can. That is the only secret of style.'[10]

Lincoln's Letters to Hooker and Grant: A Case History

One of the harder tasks of communication is to express confidence to a person while at the same time rejecting some of his words, actions or policies. Lincoln, a master of direct simple communication, demonstrated his ability to face and overcome this problem in his letter to 'Fighting Joe' Hooker. Lincoln had considerable difficulty in finding a General up to the standard necessary to beat such Confederate leaders as Robert E. Lee and 'Stonewall' Jackson. By 1863 General Wingfield Scott, the first over-all commander, and Generals McClellan and Burnside in the eastern theatre of operations, had all retired or been discarded by the President. Despite his careless conversation and insubordinate mien Hooker had commended himself to Lincoln on account of his offensive spirit. As 1863 unfolded, it became apparent that Hooker was not the man that Lincoln was looking for, but his letter is an eloquent testimony to the President's firm attempt to make the most of Hooker's strengths and to minimize his weaknesses by revealing his knowledge of them and a willingness to discount them for the sake of the common cause:

Executive Mansion,
Washington,
January 26, 1863

MAJOR GENERAL HOOKER.

GENERAL

I have placed you at the head of the Army of the Potomac. Of course, I have done this upon what appear to me to be sufficient reasons. And yet I think it best for you to know that there are some things in regard to which, I am not quite satisfied with you. I believe you to be a brave and skillful soldier, which, of course, I like. I also believe you do not mix politics with your profession, in which you are right. You have confidence in yourself, which is a valuable, if not an indispensable quality. You are ambitious, which, within reasonable bounds, does good rather than harm. But I think that during General Burnside's command of the Army, you have taken counsel of your ambition, and thwarted him as much as you could, in which you did a great wrong to the country, and to a most meritorious and honorable brother officer. I have heard, in such a way as to believe it, of your recently saying that both the Army and the Government needed a Dictator. Of course, it was not *for* this, but in spite of it, that I have given you the command. Only those generals who gain successes, can set up dictators. What I now ask of you is military success, and I will risk the dictatorship. The government will support you to the utmost of its ability, which is neither more or less than it has done and will do for all commanders. I much fear that the spirit which you have aided to infuse into the Army, of criticizing their Commander, and witholding confidence from him, will now turn upon you. I shall assist you as far as I can, to put it down. Neither you, nor Napoleon, if he were alive again, could get any good out of an army, while such a spirit prevails in it.

And now, beware of rashness. Beware of rashness, but with energy, and sleepless vigilance, go forward, and give us victories.

Yours very truly,

A. LINCOLN

By 1864 Lincoln had found his man in General Ulysses Grant. Again the President showed his consummate skill as a communicator, expressing the right balance of direction, encouragement and caution without in any way detracting from the full delegation of executive action. Like its predecessor this letter illustrates the principles of simplicity and clarity.

Executive Mansion,
Washington,
April 30, 1864

LIEUTENANT GENERAL GRANT.

Not expecting to see you again before the Spring campaign opens, I wish to express, in this way, my entire satisfaction with what you have done up to this time, so far as I understand it. The particulars of your plans I neither know or seek to know. You are vigilant and self-reliant; and, pleased with this, I wish not to obtrude any constraints or restraints upon you. While I am very anxious that any great disaster, or capture of our men in great numbers, shall be avoided, I know these points are less likely to escape your attention than they would be mine. If there is anything wanting which is within my power to give, do not fail to let me know it.

And now with a brave army, and a just cause, may God sustain you.

Yours very truly,

A. LINCOLN

CHAPTER EIGHT

THE ART OF READING

Reading maketh a full man; conference a readye man;
and writing an exacte man

FRANCIS BACON

Most professional and managerial jobs, especially those at the higher levels, have always involved much reading. Recently, despite the various onslaughts of the Prose Revolution over the last fifty years, the stacks of paperwork in organizations have steadily mounted. Correspondence, internal memoranda and technical or general reports increase every year. Moreover the manager is exhorted to read the published journals and books relevant to his general responsibility and particular industry. No wonder that courses which promise to double your reading speed have proved so popular!

Flashing screens produced by an awesome sounding machine called a tachistoscope, blinds which move down the lines of a page, films of print moving at different speeds, carefully graded exercises: these are some of the techniques evolved at Harvard University for doubling your speed from the reported adult average of 200–250 words per minute. These battery hen methods make it all look too scientific. They may also disguise the important point that *fast reading* with comprehension, although important, is only one skill in the art of reading.

Besides the ability to read fast when the situation demands it the art of reading includes another skill, which for want of a better term we can call the *skill of perusing*. Any skill involves making rapid practical decisions, many of them unconscious or habitual. The skill of perusing consists of making fast, accurate and unswerving decisions about the piece of writing in front of you. A good peruser will accurately determine what level of reading attention a piece requires, and how much of it requires, or offers to reward, close reading.

The above two skills – the tactics and strategy of fast reading – can be improved with practice. But they do not exhaust the importance of reading in training for communication. By the word 'training' I include education at this point. The difference between a trained and an educated communicator can be the same as that between 'broilers' and 'free-range' hens. In the situational limits of courses we may have to emphasize the training aspect: the interaction of theory and practice. But we shall fail if we do not point out the value of free-range reading to the person who wants to give and receive through the medium of language.

For reading plays a vital, subtle and complex part in building up the resources of people for the work of communication. The written word, for instance, gives our minds practice in analysing or sifting, synthesizing and valuing. The distinctive feature of reading lies precisely in the opportunity the written word gives us for pausing to think. When we listen we are at the mercy of the speaker; with a written piece we are more in control of the communication process.

Besides analysis we can also practice synthesis — the relation of this idea or fact to others in the corpus of our knowledge. Books or articles provide us with vicarious experience; they enable a reader to take swiftly the knowledge which the writer may have expended much of his life and many heartaches to gather. For 'A good book', wrote Milton, 'is the precious life-blood of a master spirit, embalmed and treasured up to a life beyond life.' Thus reading is one of the ways we stock up our depth minds. All kinds of information, images and ideas can be allowed to sink down through the sun-filtered waters, coated with protective layers of interest, to await in the sand for some unknown destiny. Thus reading feeds our minds, and it can give a certain quality or timbre to the voice of the man who has dined well. Or, as Bacon put it more succinctly: 'Reading maketh a full man.'

To summarize so far, there are three elements which go to make the good reader. First, he must have so mastered the technique of reading that he is towards the faster end of the continuum of technical ability. Secondly, he is skilled in judging what to read and at what depth, so that he saves much time by skimming the unimportant passages. Thirdly, he reads good books. Each of these aspects merits further examination.

Faster Reading

So important is reading for us in a civilized society that we ensure that all children capable of it master the skill in their primary and secondary education. A child starts to read slowly and aloud because he has to make decisions consciously about each word. He begins to speed up when his word recognition develops. Pronouncing the word aloud, so that he can distinguish it by the sound, becomes less necessary. The ability to read silently is the natural climax to the skill of reading, and indeed it is a comparatively recent one. In ancient times it was the practice for the literate few to read aloud, and they were probably unable to read at all without at least audibly mouthing the words. In the fifth century St Augustine of Hippo, while still a young university professor of rhetoric recorded his admiration for St Ambrose, Bishop of Milan, whom he noted – among other things – could read without moving his lips: 'his eye glided over the pages... but his voice and tongue were at rest.'[1]

One frequent symptom of a below-average-speed reader is the persistence into adulthood of lip movements or any physical throat tremors, like those of a ventriloquist. One test is to place a finger on your 'Adam's apple' and see if moves while you are reading silently. For those who do still mouth words a course in reading techniques may prove invaluable.

The average speed an educated person in the West can read without losing full comprehension of the meaning, is said to be about 200–250 words per minute, provided the subject matter is reasonably easy – a novel, say. This speed is attained by an averagely intelligent child by about the age of thirteen years; a university graduate will properly average between 300 and 500 words a minute, with some exceptional ones close to 1000 words:

> It may be thought that the slow readers grasp and retain more of what they read than do fast ones. This is not found to be the case. In general the fast readers understand and remember more of what they read. This is not the paradox that it may appear, for the slower readers are hampered all the time by the comparative inefficiency of their reading machinery, mental and physical... The reader, who can get along with such (easy) material at over eight hundred and fifty words per minute, does not always read at this speed, any more than a driver, whose car can do eighty miles an hour takes road-crossings, villages, bridges and corners at this speed.[2]

Leaving aside the last point about perusing (to be discussed in the next section) we are left with the importance of being able to read fast when the road is open and the going is easy. The considerable literature on the subject claims that our eyes move in five or six jerks along a line, pausing while we read in each 'fixation'. According to them the secret is to train the eyes to take in each line in only one or two jerks. The variety of exercises and visual aids mentioned above are designed to induce the reader to adopt this habit. Personally I do not find this advice very helpful. Once I start getting self-conscious about my eye movements I forget what I am reading about. My suggestion would be to *relax* the eye muscles, *forget* about eye jerks and let the eyes move *smoothly and evenly* along the line of words, like a scythe regularly sweeping down the long grass.

It is easy to test your speed by roping off a piece of prose, and reading it against the clock. But you have to test yourself for comprehension as well. If the material is average in difficulty, e.g. an article in a 'quality' newspaper, you should be able to read it at not less than about 300 words a minute. Arnold Bennett estimated the average book reviewer's speed at eight words per second, which gives 480 words a minute. [3] An Irish professor, doubtless training on Irish whiskey, has claimed 4,200 words per minute. If you are much slower, a full reading course, tachistoscope and all, is recommended. Or you may like to try one of the excellent Do-It-Yourself manuals on the subject. [4] But if it is a question of tuning up the engine, all that is needed is some practice — thanks to our school-teachers. For once our reading habits are set it is hard to change them. And we owe a great deal to those who taught us to read silently, swiftly and with understanding when we were young.

The Skill of Perusing

The general skill of fast and accurate reading leans only in small part on the techniques of eye movement. Indeed the difficulties of improving eye-movement habits are so considerable after years of reading that unless one is extremely slow, less than 250 words a minute, it is hardly worth the trouble. The big gains in speed can be made elsewhere. Our word *skill* probably comes from one of two Old Norse words meaning respectively to distinguish or to decide. The habitual 'decisions' or skill of co-ordinating eye movements with meaning, are one aspect of reading. The other skill lies in making accurate judgements in what to read, at what level of thoroughness. For, as Bacon reminds us, 'some books are to be read only in parts; others to read, but not curiously; and some few to be read wholly, and with diligence and attention.' [5] The skill of changing gear, and adjusting speed to the material, we might call the skill of perusing, which means to survey or scrutinize a piece of writing by reading through or over it.

The barriers against effective perusing are partly psychological. We impose rules on ourselves which are not really valid: they are relics of the classroom.

Thus the first step is to free ourselves from two such rules, which tend to be indoctrinated in us from infancy. They are:

Always start at the beginning and read through to the end.
Always move your eyes from left to right horizontally over the page (like a typewriter).

Both are good rules for those first learning to read, but they inhibit the person who wants to develop the advanced skill of perusing.

Begin by breaking the first rule. See how much you can learn about a book or report without actually reading it. The book cover and publisher's blurb (which often contains a brief summary), the intro-duction, the table of contents and the conclusion are key places for sniffing out the general scent of the book – not its actual smell, although that can be interesting enough. Survey the length and weight against one or two core-samples of the content you drill at random in the middle reaches. Gauge the author and his experience – has he something to say? By this time – four or five minutes – you should begin to know your own reactions, which will tell you whether you want to read the piece not once but several times, word by word, or merely sift through it for nuggets of wisdom.

The main danger of perusing is that speed can lead to a gradual loss of control. Like the listener, the reader's first duty is to grasp what the other person means. Depending on the ability of the writer, this can be an easy or near-impossible task. One has to stop and check frequently. Is this what he means? What is he really getting at? If one peruses too fast it is easy to misjudge a corner and end up in the ditch of culpable ignorance. 'But you *should* have read my letter more carefully...' may be the epitaph on your promotion prospects.

We are sometimes inhibited from free perusal by the second rule: the ingrained sense that *proper* reading means the jerking of the eyes so many times to the right at each line of print. Having freed ourselves from an unthinking adherence to this rule we can develop long rhythmic eye sweeps, zipping vertically down the middle of a page. Additionally we may opt for still less time and employ what the French called *coup d'oeil*, the rapid glance that takes in a whole page at a time. Margins help this movement because they act like picture frames. Indeed it is possible to imagine each page or section as a picture. Individual words are like bricks: it is the message on the wall that matters.

Occasionally or frequently the writer will trip you up and persuade you to pause over a paragraph, page or chapter. Indeed the journey may prove unexpectedly valuable, and back you go to the first page to read or re-read every sentence with a newly-kindled interest. Having rid ourselves of any shame at disobeying the law of Start At The Beginning And Go Through To The End we should be able to skip forwards or backwards, letting our perusal change from reading to skimming as it seems fit according to the signals from the page.

Abandoning these rules may seem easy, but behind them lies a certain attitude to the printed word. Books used to be rare and valuable; even today they are not cheap. They deserve respect.

Words are somehow extensions of the people who wrote them, and we feel that we should treat them with reverence. The letter writers or compilers of a report may not be 'master-spirits', but they have expended time and trouble to put down a message. Surely we should reward their labour by reading word for word what they say? As for writing on printed books, even though they belong to us... this is regarded as much a sin as inscribing graffiti on the walls of public places.

With the perusal of paper-work connected with our jobs, however, such a reverential attitude is totally out of place. The reader has to be humane but he has to mean business. Like a deckhand on an arctic trawler gutting fish he has no time to be squeamish. His knife must go in and slit the book or report down the middle, laying bare that one sentence or paragraph, which is the still-beating heart of the written piece. The idea of swiftly and skilfully gutting a book or report may seem repellent, but that is the reality of reading in a world where books, reports and articles fall on the decks of our desk in massive shoals.

So we have to rid ourselves once and for all of the idea that the reader has a moral duty to read every word when he takes up a written piece. 'What, have you not read it through?' Boswell once asked. 'No, Sir,' replied Dr Johnson, 'do *you* read books *through*?'[6]

Five Guidelines for Rapid Readers

There is no magic formula for rapid reading. The quality of early education, native abilities and much practice are the slow ascents towards fast, accurate and comprehensive reading. But — like everything else — there is always room for improvement. The summary of guidelines for self-training set out below may sound like common sense, as indeed they are, if considered individually. It is their cumulative effect which counts. At first the following of these rules will seem time-consuming. For example, it *looks* as if one saves time by plunging straight in to a book. But with practice they become habitual and

speedy:
1. Prepare by previewing the *content* of the piece which interests you – study the title, sub-headings, illustrations, and author's aims in writing.
2. Look at the author's pattern – the structure plan or *method* which he has adopted – the table of contents, rough lengths of chapters, appendices and notes.
3. Sample one or two paragraphs to test the writing – density of thought, tone, intelligibility, the 'ring of truth'.
4. Peruse (if still interested) the whole or selected parts, looking more closely for the necklace thread of the argument or theme – key paragraphs, sentences or words.
5. Develop actual reading speed with long rhythmic eye sweeps, both horizontal and vertical

Seen in this way, reading is not unlike buying and cleaning an old picture. One has to assess its value, checking the painter and date, canvas, stretcher, and frame, looking upon it as a whole. Then, having decided how much to invest and that it is worth cleaning, the transaction is made. Then the work of taking off each layer or veneer of varnish can begin. If the quality merits it, the final work may be extremely close and detailed. The end result should be: first, that the painter's original intention becomes clear in its natural colours; secondly, that the beholder has gained some kind of personal enrichment from the picture. The ability to work swiftly and deftly at these different levels – analysing here and valuing there – stands at the centre of the art of reading.

Good Reading

To delve into the contents or quality of what is to be read may seem to take us too far beyond the stated scope of this present book. In the literature on reading written for managers all the emphasis falls upon the *techniques* of faster reading. But, as we have seen, speed depends largely on a swift series of value judgements. Consequently the more that we work out our criteria of excellence in advance – before the excitement starts – the more likely we are to peruse effectively.

The word 'good' keeps cropping up. The Greeks distinguished between *kalos* and *agathos*: the former meaning good in the technical sense of being well-fitted for its work, the latter meaning good as a moral virtue. The opposite to *kalos* would be incompetent or inefficient; the reverse of *agathos* would be evil. To some extent the two areas of meanings shade into each other, like colours in a rainbow, but how far they do so is a matter for differing opinions. Perhaps we could define a good book as one which has intrinsic value for the reader and is well written at the same time. In other words it is one which simultaneously provides instruction, inspiration and pleasure.

The latter point — the dimension of delight — springs largely from the use of language. Books and articles which not only convey the message but do it gracefully are especially important in this context of communication because they create beneficial by-products in the mind of the reader which help him to be a better speaker, writer and listener. The 'message only' books fail to do this. Moreover, *their* by-products may actually warp the reader's own powers of expression. For example, good books maintain the values of language: they keep our vocabulary up to the mark, extending it naturally without tedious resort to dictionaries. Without being aware of it, something of the author's feel for language rubs off on to the reader. Books without that modest but definite flavour may provide their readers with necessary facts and figures but they will never strengthen the life-lines of human communication. They do only one job and not two. A good book costs the same (or even slightly less) than a bad one, but it is worth more because it produces two crops for the price of one.

Take the Authorized Version of the Bible as an example. Quite apart from its spiritual and moral content, the Authorized Version has had an enormous influence on the style and vocabulary of generations of the English-speaking people. Most of us use words or phrases quite unconsciously borrowed at first or second-hand from this great translation. Many preachers, politicians, trade union leaders and practical men of all kinds have echoed the cadences of the Authorized Version in their speeches. There are other examples, such as the Book of Common Prayer, Shakespeare, and Milton. In the second division we might place such writers as Bunyan, Macaulay, Scott, Hardy, Gibbon and Dickens. But the reader will be able to supplement that list with other writers or individual books which have influenced his own vocabulary and style.

Such writers make it all look effortless and easy. They take common words and use them with economy and grace. Poetry makes good reading for business men because a poem is complete and concise. In great poetry it is possible to see what language can do in a tight space when it dances to the tune of a master. After all, in the history of the world we should find poéts among the top twenty 'communicators' of all time. It is a pity that we have built up this division between common everyday writing and 'fine art' literature, fencing poetry around with all kinds of reverential taboos. After all, the word poet only comes from the Greek verb 'to make' or 'to manufacture'. The poet is cousin to the industrialist.

Books which established their excellence both for content and language used to be known as 'classics', a standing compliment to the ancient Greek and Roman authors. Every field of human interest now has the classics. The path to good reading surely does not lie in forcing oneself to swallow daily doses of such 'model' writers as Macaulay or Gibbon but to start from a present field of interest and find out what books have established their reputations in that area. In management studies, for example, the logic of interest leads us to such writers as Douglas McGregor and Peter Drucker. Beside the content of their books – which is simple without being simplistic – one can admire their lively and pleasing styles, the way they deploy their arguments and sustain the readers' interest throughout.

Reading books with established reputations does save time. But one does need to keep a sense of adventure. There is much to be said for browsing in bookshops and public libraries, or on other people's shelves. The portly Dr Johnson relished browsing. On one visit, having been ushered into the host's library, he 'ran eagerly to one side of the room, intent on poring over the backs of the books', explaining: 'When we inquire into any subject, the first thing we have to do is to know what books have treated of it. This leads us to look at catalogues and the backs of books in libraries.'[7]

History and biography are fields of reading which hold hidden treasures for all those who must exercise leadership in organizations. Owing to changes in the situation, it is not possible to learn universally applicable lessons from the history books or lives of great men. But we can add to our store of knowledge. Moreover, history prods our creative thinking. The inter-play of personalities, events and situations, the *story* of what actually happened, makes compelling reading, especially if we can see links or connections with our own experience. In more practical matters history develops our sense of why things happen the way they do. History is about people. It helps us to understand people at work, with their living values and driving needs, and to see how our human nature both remains constant and seems to alter like a chameleon against its historical or social background.

It is tempting to restrict such reading to what promises to be 'relevant' history. For example, a business man may choose to read only industrial histories, or a soldier confine himself to military history, hoping thereby to ensure interest and profit. But professional narrowness attends such restrictions of interest. It is much better to read more widely, while observing certain limits. A business man may learn more about people under stress, for example, from Ernle Bradford's account of the 71-year-old Knight Hospitaller La Vallete's leadership in the Great Siege of Malta (1565) than from many a commissioned firm's history! Doubtless, as the writing of business history improves, there will be better books nearer home for him to enjoy.[8]

The leader at any level may discover more about the realities of organizational politics — a dimension which seems to escape most social scientists — from writers long dead, as Anthony Jay has suggested in his entertaining and thought-provoking book entitled *Management and Machiavelli* (1967).[9] Commercial and industrial enterprise has its roots in history, and to understand any phenomenon it is essential to know the story of its growth and development within the context of the wider human story.

Lastly, it is possible to over-emphasize the differences between organizational life, especially in their higher reaches. Walter Bagehot has written in *The English Constitution*:

> The summits of the various kinds of business are, like the tops of mountains, much more alike than the parts below — the bare principles are much the same; it is only the rich variegated details of the lower strata that so contrast with one another. But it needs travelling to know that the summits *are* the same. Those who live on one mountain believe that *their* mountain is wholly unlike all others.[10]

Conclusion

We tend to take reading for granted, and to look upon it as the 'easy' part of communication. A symptom of this underestimation is the exclusive concentration on reading *speed*, coupled with the equation of reading with a mechanical technique, that characterizes the attention given to it in many adult training courses and educational centres. But reading plays a much more interesting and complex part in the total economy of communication than these 'rapid reading' techniques suggest.

We learn most of our reading abilities as children. It is possible, however, for an adult to increase his reading speed if it is average or less than average. Usually this entails correcting some bad habit, such as lip moving, which a good teacher should have spotted long ago. Command of vocabulary and plenty of practice should lead naturally to a higher reading speed.

The skill of perusing is a vital element in the art of reading. Knowing what to leave out without detriment to the aim in reading can lead to the rapid despatch of reading, although the mechanical speed of one's eye movement may not be much faster than a plodding neighbour. Some books require reading sentence by sentence, but perusing, skimming or scanning is more often demanded, especially as the pyramid of paperwork mounts ever higher.

Finally the deeper fruits of reading can only be achieved if there is quality in the books or articles one reads. Physical reading, like all communicatory abilities, is only a method. It is the contents which alone can enrich the mind and inform action. Wide-ranging reading is important because it stimulates the imagination and stocks up our depth or unconscious minds. Indeed, as Descartes wrote, 'the reading of all the good books is like having a conversation with the highly worthy persons of the past who wrote them; indeed, it is like having a prepared conversation in which those persons disclose to us only their best thinking.'

Thus the art of reading is that harmony of skills which enables the communicant to seize upon the worthwhile and valuable through the medium of the written or printed word. To that end he must feed on the better books, so that he recognizes quality when he sees it in the more ephemeral reading he tackles in the bustle of a busy office or the crush of a commuter train. Like all the best arts it is one which we never completely master. And, like them, it yields us both profit and pleasure.

CHAPTER NINE

MEETINGS: THE CHAIRMAN AS A LEADER

He that complies against his will
Is of his own opinion still.

Hudibras, SAMUEL BUTLER

From the preceding chapter it is evident that a manager or leader in any kind of organization is going to find himself in the 'hot seat' as chairman or initiator at a whole range of meetings: briefing groups, consultations, committees and conferences. Managing the exchange of information and ideas has become a vital aspect of leadership in contemporary society. More than that, the leader must seek and direct a true union of minds, wills and actions.

The work of leaders in any setting is the provision of the necessary functions to achieve the common task, to build the team and to meet the needs of its individual members. These needs, present in the whole organization and in its more permanent groups, are also alive briefly in the *ad hoc* working parties, meetings or committees with which we are concerned at this point. But there are no invisible boundaries around the meeting room: the wider needs and values of the organization will invade the small group discussion, and what the leader has, or has not done in the larger setting will influence the *ad hoc* meeting for good or ill.

Whether the leader is appointed, elected or emergent (or some combination of these possibilities), he still has to prepare for the meeting and exercise positive leadership within it. The principle of Be Prepared includes thinking about the organizational context of the forthcoming meeting: why it is being held, who is coming and what is to be discussed or decided. A key question is how far the meeting is concerned with actually taking a decision, rather than with airing views, making suggestions, stimulating creative ideas, or exchanging information.

If the group is to be concerned with decision making it is important to be clear from the off-set about the relative 'shares' which the leader and the group members will have in the decision.[1] For example, a policy decision may have been made by the main board and the heads of departments called together to co-ordinate their implementing of that decision. In other words, although the group may not share in the actual decision, there is plenty of room for participating in the lesser but still major decisions on how to realize the policy in the most effective, efficient and satisfying way.

The main functions necessary to meet the three areas of leadership responsibility are the same for any purposeful activity, but the meeting situation does call for particular applications of them, such as the skills of clarifying, summarizing and testing for consensus. Consequently it is worthwhile to consider briefly the main functions of leadership in relation to the management of information, ideas and decisions.

The leader is responsible for the provision of such functions, but that does not mean he supplies them all himself. Indeed he cannot do so. If the group members have had opportunities in training to develop their own natural awareness, understanding and skill as leaders, they should be better able to supplement and buttress the work of the appointed or elected leader in all three over-lapping areas of responsibility. Paradoxically if people aim at becoming better leaders they cannot help becoming better followers, because they can use their knowledge and experience to complement and support the man or woman who carries the main burden of accountability. On the other hand, the provision of at least the essential parts of the general leadership functions by one person does save time, leaving the other members free to devote all their 10,000 million or more brain cells to the matter in hand.

INITIATING

Be it a single decision or a series of them, the exchange of opinions or the stirring of the creative depth mind, a meeting is usually about something. In the early stages it is fitting for the leader to state (or perhaps re-state) *what* the meeting is for and *why* it is necessary, valuable or desirable.

It should not be supposed, however, that this function can be performed satisfactorily by a ritual incantation at the start of the proceedings. Despite a lack of comments, questions or interruptions from them in those initial opening minutes members may voice their uncertainties about the aim or objective of the discussions at any point in the meeting. The leader should not be surprised or annoyed by such interventions. All of us, at some time or another, have lacked the courage to say that we do not know what it is all about, especially when everyone else seems quite happy. If time allows, the leader should counter these doubts with a succinct re-formulation of the task and the relevant constraints. Or, if the failure lies in the vocabulary of the leader, it may be that somebody else can interpret the objective into language which the hesitant person can grasp.

Wise leaders anticipate these delayed reactions by checking for comprehension. In other words, they seek early feedback on the success or failure of their efforts at conveying the objective of the meeting and the values implicit in it. 'Any questions?' is one direct method. But it is always profitable to supplement this question with a swift glance at the faces around. Often the feelings which accompany uncertainty or doubt find expression in the looks of people, and a leader should open himself to these non-verbal communications which fill the air as invisibly as radio music. One way of helping a leader is by not assuming a poker face, or — even worse — a mask of smiling and positive assent, when inwardly there is nothing but mental fog. At this early stage some *dialogue* — spoken or glanced — is essential.

The only test of how well the objective or intention of the meeting has been explained is the result or outcome of the discussion and subsequent action. If the group charges — like the Light Brigade at Balaclava — in the wrong direction, and finishes up in total disintegration as an assortment of angry or frustrated individuals, we may be reasonably certain that the leader fell at the first functional hurdle.

Incidentally, during the Crimean War battle at Inkerman, the 'thin red line' of British soldiers frequently drove back hordes of Russians. Many of the latter fell down, pretending to be dead, and the British soldiers — returning to their own heights in the mist — encountered these 'resurrection boys', as they called them, scampering back to the Russian positions. There are 'resurrection boys' in committee meetings: members who assent vocally to the objective and then 'jump up' later, showing that they were only pretending to agree. The leader may be forgiven if he succumbs to more irritation in re-stating the objective for these 'resurrection boys', who must of course be distinguished from those who genuinely thought that they had understood, but only subsequently discover that they had not checked their listening sufficiently well.

PLANNING
Once the task is seen and accepted a plan is needed. A plan means the allocation of resources in the constraints of time and space to achieve an aim or objective. Thus a plan is a way of structuring the meeting, so

that it tackles the work in hand with order. To use a musical analogy, the function of planning may be compared to hammering out a musical score which orchestrates a theme; so that all the talents and contributions of the group's players are integrated to the maximum effect within the available time.

Making a plan involves decisions about the framework or skeleton of the meeting. Again it is important for the leader to think out in advance how much participation in these decisions of method would be appropriate. Sometimes he may announce all the plan; sometimes he may be willing to go along with almost any plan providing that it promises to command the assent and whole-hearted involvement of the group's members. But he cannot evade his responsibility for ensuring that there is some workable plan adopted or accepted for the meeting.

Planning can never be a mechanical function. It depends as much upon the valuing faculty of the mind as the analysing and synthesizing abilities. For a plan should reflect the priorities of the task: what *must* be done, what *should* be done and what *might* be done. According to Aneurin Bevan '75 per cent of political wisdom is a sense of priorities', and that is true about planning. Without this sense of priorities a plan can easily become rigid and inflexible, for priorities can change in a shifting situation and the leader has to watch them all the time. Establishing these priorities and retaining an awareness of them, however, prevents such over-planning, which can be as damaging as under-planning.

Another activity naturally associated with planning is the allocation of sub-tasks or functions by the leader to group members. Sometimes the custom or practice of the organization or society will have already ensured that certain minimal tasks will be performed, e.g. taking notes or minutes. But the leader should always check these arrangements. In addition he may delegate jobs to others where this is appropriate.

Planning may well include – explicitly or implicitly – the establishing of work standards or norms. These are the stated or informal rules which can eliminate a lot of unnecessary discussion or work. For example, one such method of working would be the parliamentary practice of addressing all remarks to the chair. A less formal example would be the rule that if possible speakers are not interrupted, or the injunction to keep contributions brief and to the point.

The leader's responsibility for planning starts before the meeting in question begins. By using his common sense, laced with some visual imagination, he should be able to foresee what will be required in or near the place of meeting. In particular he ought to look at the seating arrangements, because sometimes these can impose their own (often unwelcome) pattern on the exchange of information and ideas, as one of King James I's chief ministers — Francis Bacon — observed over three hundred years ago:

> A long table and a square table, or seats about the walls, seem things of form, but are things of substance; for at a long table a few at the upper end, in effect, sway all the business; but in the other form there is more use of the counsellors' opinions that sit lower. A king, when he presides in council, let him beware how he opens his own inclination too much in that which he propoundeth; for else counsellors will but take the wind of him, and, instead of giving free counsel, will sing him a song of 'I shall please'.[2]

CONTROLLING

The function of controlling describes the pattern of words and actions which keep the discussion on course. Any group of people talking is liable to follow red herrings, or to linger on the easier slopes rather than pushing on to the heights. An effective group, however, will not need much spurring or whipping: a slight pressure, a subtle hint or even a look will suffice to re-unite it with the objective of the meeting.

Sometimes unruly members, inflamed by strong feelings, may ignore even these gentle signals. Or a veteran bore may seize the group by the throat. In such situations a firm but friendly exercise of the controlling function is expected or required from the chairman. A touch of humour can sweeten the sharp medicine. This point is well illustrated by the practice of the present Speaker of the House of Commons, Mr Selwyn Lloyd:

> One of the most useful weapons in a Speaker's armoury is a sense of humour and a wit which, if used in the correct way and at the right moment, can bring the Commons to heel like a hunting horn with a pack of hounds. Those who did not know Mr Lloyd well a year ago suspected that he would be found wanting in this respect. How mistaken they were. Time and again during the past year the Speaker's dry wit has thrust home to take the sting out of many a nasty situation or to deflate pomposity.
>
> Once, when Mr Wilson and Labour MPs were in hot pursuit of Mr Heath over his yachting activities and the exchanges across the table were getting more and more bitter and less and less relevant, with talk about half-time Prime Ministers, Mr Lloyd intervened to tell the House: 'I think it is time we got back on to the fairway.' The

reference to Mr Wilson's golfing pursuits was not lost on MPs and when the laughter from both sides had died down, the Commons returned at once to more serious matters.

The leader at industrial meetings, even at shop-floor bargaining encounters, will rarely face the difficulties faced by the Speaker, for political passions run high and can erupt into physical violence or threats thereof during the long debates. Yet any chairman, manager or trade union official has to be able to exercise control without appearing to be autocratic or insensitive. Again a good reputation will aid him. Certainly Mr Selwyn Lloyd's experience in Parliament had given him the right sort of credit.

His spell as Leader of the House earned him a high reputation for reasonableness and fairness and he was recognized as having the interests of the Commons always at heart. It was the regard of his fellow MPs gained when he was leader which had much to do with setting the seal on his election last year.

Remembering at all times that his powers stem from the Commons themselves, he must control the House in a way that is never dictatorial. Mr Lloyd does this superbly, with just the right touch of natural modesty to crush the most arrogant intervention. [3]

Sarcasm, facetiousness or slighting remarks are inappropriate methods of controlling the path of a discussion. Nor does any form of hectoring or bullying contribute much to task achievement, team maintenance or the individual needs of members. These blunt weapons inflict grievous wounds and produce no good results. Far better is a quiet reminder of the time constraints, a firm tone of voice or a re-statement of the problem or decision which lies on the table.

Lord Attlee, when Prime Minister, exemplified many of the attributes of a good chairman in these respects and later wrote:

The Prime Minister shouldn't speak too much himself in Cabinet. He should start the show or ask somebody else to do so, and then intervene only to bring out the more modest chaps who, despite their seniority, might say nothing if not asked. And the Prime Minister must sum up... Particularly when a non-Cabinet Minister is asked to attend, especially if it is his first time, the Prime Minister may have to be cruel. The visitor may want to show how good he is, and go on too long. A good thing is to take no chance and ask him to send the Cabinet a paper in advance... If somebody else looks like making a speech, it is sound to nip in with, 'Are you *objecting*?

You're not? Right. Next business', and the Cabinet can move on.[4]

One important way of guiding the discussion is to *summarize* progress so far, so that the remaining issues or agenda stand out clearly. Thus a summary given during a meeting (rather than in conclusion) can act as a trumpet sounding the recall. But the summary has to be accurate, simple, clear and vivid. With all his other responsibilities it requires a high level of natural ability and practice for a leader to be able to summarize succinctly at the right time, in such a way that the summary is instantly accepted as a true account of the proceedings to date.

Although summarizing is an especially important skill for a chairman, all listeners can find it useful on occasions. A summary is a sign of listening because it establishes whether or not a communicant can select the salient points to the satisfaction of the speaker and the rest of the audience, if there is one. A summary not only chops away much of the dead-wood and foliage, but it also provides a listening check, for other listeners will either accept your abbreviation or reject it. Thus a summary helps the process of thought and digestion.

The singer, however, takes a piano note and transforms it into a vocal sound. Another chairmanship asset is the distinctively human ability to *interpret* from one language into another, without loss of fidelity to the original. The interpreter must be able to divine meaning and translate it into a different language. For example, an economic spokesman may have to translate a difficult complex financial matter into language simple enough to be understood by laymen with reasonable effort. His ability to do so will test his powers as a listener. But a timely interpretation can contribute to the over-all direction of the discussion.

SUPPORTING

Supporting is a general or portmanteau word for a host of minor functions which give a group a sense of being a team while at the same time enhancing the value of individuals and maximizing their personal contribution. Quite literally supporting means to strengthen the position of a person or community by one's assistance, countenance or adherence. Supporting covers all those words and actions of encouragement which sustain organizations, groups or individuals in testing times or circumstances.

Groups as wholes are always stronger than the sum of their individual parts. The social force of feeling and opinion is so powerful that grown men can fall sick and die if they are ostracized by their fellows. Indeed in primitive societies to turn your face away from someone is a severe punishment. For we need people who will 'countenance' us, or turn a friendly face towards us. In groups we remain aware of these primeval forces in our depth minds: hence the shades of our reactive feelings, which range from shyness through to a proper respect for the power of the community.

For this reason individuals may find it difficult to speak their minds in groups. The leader, who has a certain counter-balancing power vis-à-vis the group, can support the individual in a variety of ways. For example, he can act as a door-keeper, noticing a silent individual and checking with him, verbally or by a quizzing look, whether or not he wants to contribute in speech. This would be the reverse of the parliamentary practice of 'catching the Speaker's eye'. During and after his contribution a speaker may well need a sustaining atmosphere of interest and encouragement. Of course not everyone has to speak at a meeting; there are plenty of ways of sharing and contributing without opening one's mouth. But people should feel free to talk if they wish, and to know that the leader will support them against, if necessary, the combined power of the group.

The leader may also respond to the group's need for maintenance and support in the teeth of difficulties. Common enterprises are fraught with natural hazards, and even a one-hour committee meeting can have its quota of despondent moments. Some meetings seem to take place in Doubting Castle under the gloomy presidency of Giant Despair. The calmness of the leader and his confidence in the fundamental goodness of the group can sustain it in its trials, just as the greater resources of faith and hope released in any meeting of true minds will both refresh and encourage the leader.

Of all necessary functions in our corporate life, supporting is the one most open to full participation. The response of a group to individual speakers is a sure sign of how far it is holding a positive and creative philosophy or set of values. With a smile or a glance one member can support another, and each can do his bit to maintain a cohesive but easy unity of relationship as well as purpose. By setting a high standard by his own listening, for example, a leader can encourage others to listen in a business-like yet positive way.

INFORMING

The function of informing concerns the import of relevant information into a group, and the passing of information from a group. It touches upon the role of a leader as a representative of the group or organization, either informally or as an appointed delegate, which role has as a corollary the bringing back of information from those other councils.

In briefing groups and joint consultations this function of leadership has pride of place. In the former the leader is passing down information (directives, policies, facts, rules etc.) to a meeting; in the latter he is gathering facts, ideas and opinions for upwards or sideways transmission. Part of his skill in performing the function lies in the ability to interpret information into a form suitable for the new audience without any loss of central meaning or intended overtones, or the addition of any unintended glosses or flavours.

Except in management and union negotiations, where the meetings may need a sequence of a constant flow of information in the shape of reactions from their parent groups to new proposals, the leader can perform this function mainly before or after the planned discussion. In other words he can ensure that the necessary information is available or easily attainable. And, secondly, he can work out how the information gathered at a meeting will find its appropriate destinations.

Thus the leader passes freely over the boundary or frontier of a group in that he may have to speak for or from it as an ambassador or impart information into it. Of course this function may be delegated to a group member, or shared in rotation. But the leader of the organization retains responsibility for this function and usually participates fairly fully in it. During the course of a meeting he is the natural communication channel for messages flowing either into a group or out of it. More than a channel, he may have to filter what should be reported to the meeting, or be allowed to pass from it before the conclusion of the discussion.

EVALUATING

Evaluating means testing the worth or value of something. We may usefully distinguish between 'quantifiable evaluation', where there is some measure or yard-stick which can be applied, and 'quality evaluation' involving a judgement based on a set of (individually) imperfect criteria. In most organizations or groups someone has to evaluate the proceedings, otherwise there is no way of knowing whether or not the task is being achieved.

Within the context of small group meetings the leader shares responsibility with the other members for testing their conclusions against certain standards or values. It may be necessary for the leader to spell out these standards, or they may be implicit. In most cases there is a mixture of explicit and semi-implicit criteria which measures the quality of the content of the communication.

Where decisions are to be taken the general function of evaluating includes checking the feasibility of proposals against the accepted values. Thus this function may involve the rational and practical activity of testing the consequences of a proposed course or solution. In groups which are seeking to stimulate creative ideas and suggestions such valuing should be tentative or even temporarily suspended altogether, for constant appraisal inhibits the shy denizens of our creative depth minds.

An important skill, which changes this general function into the small coinage of detailed action, is *testing for commitment*. Not all decisions should be made by consensus, or even by majority vote, but in a democratic society many should be. Moreover the closer a group comes to consensus the more its members will tend to feel involved, committed or responsible for the outcome. Consensus, incidentally, does not mean total 100 per cent agreement on the part of each individual. Rather consensus stands for the decision which everyone will accept and go along with as the best in the circumstances. In physiology it means the general accord of different organs of the body in effecting a given purpose.

Some leaders possess a natural awareness of the consentive feeling in a group; others develop it over a life-time. Of course, knowing where the consensus lies does not necessarily mean that the leader accepts the group direction. He may seek to change, or influence it, or — in the last resort — tender his resignation. But whatever his ultimate response it is a good start for him if he can sense the invisible consensus. Groups, like moving shoals of fish, have an unseen centre point; a constantly shifting pole which draws the fish together as if by magnetic influence. Consensus in human groups is a similar centre of feelings. No leader can afford to be so oblivious of this point or so far ahead of it that all contact is lost.

Thus, like Moses, the leader has to know when and where to strike the water of consensus from the rock of outward appearance. It is not always evident where the water lies, and the leader of any meeting should be able to test for consensus. Like water divining, this is an inexact science. It is made up of simultaneously asking for people's views while watching their faces and expressions. Views may be elicited either by direct questions, or else putting forward a trial consensus and judging the reactions. In this case testing for consensus is akin to summarizing.

What has to be avoided like the plague is a mistaken assumption about group consensus, made from a misinterpretation of one or two nods or smiles, a few murmurs of approval or the out-pourings of a voluble self-appointed spokesman. When the leader seizes upon such straws he either reveals his incompetence or (even worse) his own wishful thinking about the result. Worst of all, it may look as if he is seeking to impose his own will by underhand methods.

The process of finding consensus is fraught with hazards, especially if some sort of consentive action is desperately needed. In particular the leader may have to guard against unfair pressures being brought to bear on individuals. 'We do *all* agree, don't we Mr Jones...' As the clock warns that the end of the meeting is nigh it is common for waves of hostile or angry feelings, separated by troughs of honeyed smiles, to wash against the opposition in a last attempt to wear it away. Like the false prophets, such groups show themselves anxious 'to cry Peace, Peace, where there is no peace'.

In the absence of consensus some groups or organizations may have alternative systems for making up their minds. The most common of these is voting. Depending on the rules, a vote may be carried either by a simple majority, even if it is only one, or else a pre-determined proportion, e.g. two-thirds, or even 75 per cent. This method is said to have the disadvantage that it leaves an unconvinced minority. But this is mitigated where the minority, having had their say, are willing to go along with the majority decision and do their best to make it work. Where they will not the leader has to balance the disruption of the group against the gains stemming from the majority decision. Such conflicts between the values of unity and harmony on the one hand, and the onwards call to advance on the other hand, can cause leaders of all ranks and shades in an organization many thoughtful hours, and there are no easy answers.

Whether or not the leader should initiate or co-operate in an evaluation of the way the group has worked together — its relationships and performance — depends upon the kind of group and the situation. In the training setting it would be natural to do so. If the committee, working party or consultative group is a standing one, then some time could profitably be spent on the analysis of 'process' as opposed to 'content', because it may lead to more effective performance 'the next time'. But such evaluation requires a delicate touch; it has to strike a balance between protecting individuals against too much or too unskilled' feedback and an unwelcome form of paternalism which consists of over-protection of the group or the individual in the face of unpleasant facts.

So much for the six basic functions of leadership in small group meetings. Each is essential. None may be performed exclusively by the leader. All are his responsibility.

CONFERENCE LEADERSHIP

A conference is simply the bringing together of a number of people for a serious (but not necessarily solemn) conversation. For my purposes I should define it as a group which must sub-divide in order to enable communication to take place. It is easy to have a discussion in which everyone is able to participate if there are less than a score of people. If there are many more, however, it is best to sub-divide into small groups for at least part of the time. The art of planning a good conference lies largely in blending the small-group and plenary sessions to perfection.

The old-style conference which consisted of a series of lectures or speeches from the platform, followed by questions from the floor, has died a peaceful death. Its *alter ego*, the 'informal' or 'structureless' conference, which floated like an amoeba in a sea of chaos, has also largely fallen out of fashion. We are left with the conviction that if one looks after the essential ingredients of structure, then the outcome of the conference will almost look after itself. These ingredients include thorough preparation and planning, followed by a flexible leadership which allows for changes in the programme if they become necessary.

Preparation includes choosing the right subject, delegates and speakers. Naturally it overlaps with planning, which centres first on the programme and ends with the last administrative details. It is at this stage that the balance between small-group work and plenary sessions has to be achieved. The pattern of 'lecture – questions – small groups – plenary report-backs' should never be regarded as fixed and inevitable. The sequence of 'small group – plenary discussion – lecture – questions' may be much more appropriate, especially in subjects where the delegates or members already have considerable knowledge or experience.

All conferences should have some sort of 'wash-up' at the end. A plenary session gathering the threads together is usually needed. Not infrequently such a session will soundly test the leader's powers of summarizing and establishing consensus. Moreover he will have to support the conference in the face of its impending physical disintegration, always difficult when the meetings have been conspicuously enjoyable and successful. This may entail an evocation of the purpose which sustains the enterprise, consciously or unconsciously, and which threads all meetings together, like pearls on a string, so that they form a progression and a unity.

LEADERSHIP MANNER

Manner, derived distantly from the Latin word *manus*, a hand, means primarily 'mode of handling', or the way in which something is done or takes place. It used to embrace the meanings of our present words for moral conduct and character, but this flavour has faded into the background. In leadership, as in any other aspect of living, it is not only *what* is done or said but *how* it is said or done which is important. How the six leadership functions are done can vividly communicate non-verbally what the leader really thinks about the relative values of task, the group, individuals and himself.

It is a pity that the phrase 'leadership styles' has become so inter-twined with the attempt to prove that one degree of participation in decision-making is 'better' than any other. As many recent writers have suggested, the appropriate 'shares' in a decision depend (or should depend) upon the situation, the subordinates and the kind of organization which forms the matrix for the group. It is regrettable also that the expression 'leadership styles' conjures up the unconvincing efforts of psychologists and sociologists to place leaders into such imaginary or over-simplified categories as Authoritarian, Autocratic, Bureaucratic, Democratic or Charismatic. In fact style is an individual matter, and it is always unique if one looks close enough. We should firmly resist the idea that leaders (or anyone else) should be 'styled' like motor cars.

On the other hand, just as certain general architectural styles seem to belong with or reflect an age, it may be that there is a wide style or manner which strikes a chord in a generation. This may be a national phenomenon, or it may be shared between certain nations or cultures. If so, it is little more than a reflection of the general principle that a leader tends to (or should) personify the qualities which are necessary or admired in a group, organization or society. Even if he does not possess them they may be ascribed to him by a grateful public.

From the leader's point of view it is important to remember that his manner will exert influence as well as the necessary functions he performs. Like the mannerisms of a public speaker, the manner of a leader is expressive of personality: it gives away at least some of the contents of his depth mind. The only remedy is to endeavour to make one's manner reflect those inner convictions beliefs and values.

Conclusion

Effective communication in any organization or society implies a number of meetings. These may vary in purpose and sail under many different flags: briefing groups, committees, joint consultations, creative 'brainstorming' sessions, and conferences — to name but a few. Yet they all require some form of leadership. For any inter-personal communication has to be managed in the right way if it is to achieve the desired results.

In the meeting situation some or all of the general leadership functions will be required, namely initiating, planning, controlling, supporting, informing and evaluating. The principles which govern how far these should be shared are well-known, and it is possible to conclude that good leadership will ensure that members participate as fully as possible in the response to task, team and individual needs.

Lastly, the leader's manner may do as much if not more than his words to encourage (or discourage) genuine communication. Humour, modesty and firmness have their own part to play. As the leader's own task encompasses the creation of a warm, friendly but business-like atmosphere it is vital that he too should check whether or not his manner aids and abets him in promoting good communication.

Perhaps the sixth century B.C. poet Lao-tzu sums up well the necessary direction and manner of leadership for today in these lines:

A leader is best
When people barely know that he exists,
Not so good when people obey and acclaim him,
Worst when they despise him.
'Fail to honour people,
They fail to honour you';
But of a good leader, who talks little,
When his work is done, his aim fulfilled,
They will all say, 'We did this ourselves.'

CHAPTER TEN

INTERVIEWS: APPRAISING – AND BEING APPRAISED

Thus they in mutual accusation spent
The fruitless hours, neither self-condemning.

JOHN MILTON

Milton's evocation of the verbal strife between Adam and Eve after their expulsion from the Garden of Eden in *Paradise Lost* may sound echoes in an experienced manager's mind. Owing to our 'fallen' human nature it is all too easy for an appraisal interview, in which one person attempts to point out to another his short-comings and failings, to develop into a Miltonian slanging match of attack and counter-attack, accusation and defence. Moreover with the growth of 'management by objectives' much more emphasis is now being placed on the formal appraisal interview, designed to assess work performance at regular intervals. Too often the 'how-to-do-it' handbooks on appraisal interviews only stress the formal aspects: the value of organizing and regularizing what is in fact a natural feature of good leadership. They ignore the major problems of communication in such situations; they overlook the common experience that the giving and receiving of praise or criticism comes highest on the list of difficult conversations.

Of course all interviews count as forms of communication, and it would be quite legitimate to include a discussion of them in a book with this title. But the essential problem of the selection interview – making a judgement about a person – has already been discussed in the companion volume in this series *Training for Decisions* (1971) where there may be found suggestions for further reading on interviewing in general. Nor do I want to go too deeply into the mechanics of appraisal interviews as part of the 'control system' in large organizations, for this departure would take us too far into the field of general management. Here I propose to concentrate on the exchange of praise and criticism, those precious but unstable commodities which can make or break individuals, teams and even organizations. Moreover it would be a mistake to limit the consideration of them entirely to the formal appraisal interview: we may find ourselves dealing in praise or criticism – on the sending or receiving end – at any time of the day or night and at any place, be it the board room or the wash-room or at home!

Before plunging into some 'Do's and 'Don'ts' it is worth recalling once again the Communication Star on p. 25. Where the 'content' is going to be praise or criticism, then the *situation* and the *method* become especially important. Who likes to be told off by the boss in front of others or at a social gathering? Who enjoys having a list of one's personal faults sent through the post or on an internal memo? Yet most important of all is the 'line of relationship' between communicator and communicant. If that is weak, broken or nonexistent, then the 'mutual accusations' will indeed spring up like flames, crackling in the dry tinder of mistrust.

Also it is worth adding that the success of this kind of communication – as all others – depends in part on the quality of the communicant or receiver. As the writer of *Proverbs* noted: 'He who corrects a scoffer gets himself abuse, and he who reproves a wicked man incurs injury. Do not reprove a scoffer, or he will hate you; reprove a wise man and he will love you. Give instruction to a wise man and he will be still wiser...'[1] A good recipient or communicant is essential if there is to be any genuine praise or constructive criticism at all.

The 'praise' in 'appraisal' comes from a Latin verb meaning to set a price or value on something. Thus Thomas Caxton in one of the first printed books could write: 'They preysed nothing the thinges that were erthely.' Our verb 'to prize' approximates it. Evaluating means virtually the same as appraising. Elsewhere I have suggested that valuing (along with analysing and synthesizing) is one of the fundamental movements of our minds: we cannot avoid doing it without an effort, and then only for very short times. Thus appraisal or evaluation lies on the trade routes of our minds quite naturally.

Praise implies a positive evaluation of worth, excellence or merit which is communicated. Like praise, criticism was originally a neutral word, and this meaning survives in the phrase 'literary criticism'. Stemming from the Greek word for a judge, it has arrived at a sense of a 'guilty' verdict, a negative evaluation. Most people are aware, however, of the distinction between 'constructive' and 'negative' criticism, the former being accompanied by suggestions for improvement.

SOME EFFECTS OF APPRAISAL
Whether governed by conscious intention or not praise and criticism can produce certain effects in the task, team and individual areas of

need present in organizations or groups. It is helpful to a leader to be aware of these results, because it may give him understanding of how easily misinterpretations of the intentions behind his comments can arise.

First, appraisal can produce guidance or control of individuals or groups. Good parents naturally employ praise in this way, as the only kind of reward they can give to very small children for such acts as cleaning up the bathroom and brushing their teeth. In adult life praise continues to be employed – consciously or unconsciously – as a natural method of getting people to conform, develop, change or work along the lines which are deemed necessary by the communicator. But if praise words are only used in this way they begin to lose their meaning; they become merely clichés or encouraging noises. Or they may be interpreted as signs of paternalism.

Secondly, in the team maintenance circle, appraisal may be interpreted by either party as an outward expression or confirmation of a relationship between their two roles. If the role implications are resented by one of them, then the temperature of the conversation may well rise rapidly. For praise or criticism implies a judgement, and the act of judging can bring home the status and rights of both the praiser as the senior and the praised as the junior.

Those who use praise or criticize solely to emphasize their superiority may soon become conspicuous because in turn they resent praise or apparent criticism being given to them by *their* superiors, let alone 'co-ordinates' or subordinates in less formal settings than the appraisal interview. The practice of 'damning with faint praise' is another weapon in their armoury. Praise or criticism from such sources, with an implied personal superiority and concious or unconscious air of condescension, often arouses rejection and hostility in the communicant; indeed can be perceived as insults.

In moderation, however, the giving of praise or evaluation may be a reinforcement of the necessary framework of working relationships, a pleasing sign of concern and care. And, of course, the situation is transformed if the communicant acknowledges the communicator's professional superiority or experience in the given area. What student composer would not have glowed at a compliment from Mozart, that king of musicians? What painter would not have taken seriously a suggestion for improving a technique if it came from Leonardo da Vinci?

Thirdly, praise or criticism may be felt as a personal reward or a punishment by the recipient. But there are managers who exploit the natural effect of praise by relying entirely on the warm drug-like influence of kind words to avoid offering more money, promotion, better opportunities or improved conditions. In the long run the credibility of such praising is called into question, for the human heart naturally looks for concrete evidences – non-verbal signs – to follow or accompany words of rewarding praise. When they could be given but are not, then we begin to suspect the speaker's sincerity. Action and speech should walk hand in hand. 'Don't talk of love – show me!'

GIVING AND RECEIVING APPRAISAL

Although appraising can produce these triple effects in groups and organizations, we should not suppose that they are always consciously in the mind of the leader. We should distinguish between *intentions* and *effects* or *consequences*. Many desirable consequences are by-products of activities directed towards other ends, and so it is with praise and criticism. What is important is that the leader should recognize and measure value when he sees it. Secondly, he should be able to express that value in words or gestures accurately, simply, clearly, vividly and naturally when the occasion calls for it. In other words he should do no more than mirror the value that is already in the work, so that the performer can see it more clearly. If he does this, then the three functions of appraisal will largely look after themselves.

Most praise and criticism is rightly directed towards performance, or what a man *does* rather than what he *is*. On the other hand the distinction between doing and being is a fluid one: to some extent our actions are fruits of our character, and our character is the by-product of our actions. 'The bird carries the wings, and the wings support the bird', as the proverb says. It is fatally easy, however, to draw false conclusions about character from observations of a person's work.

As a general rule, for that reason, it is often suggested that appraisal conversations should stop short at comments about performance, and eschew any reactions to character. But there are obvious exceptions to such a common-sense rule. We all need a certain balance of self-esteem. That balance is always shifting. Sometimes we respect our own conduct or stance; sometimes we feel guilty and despise ourselves; sometimes we fall into bouts of self-pity. In the hours when our proper level of self-confidence is slipping a good leader or friend may deftly and tactfully restore our sense of self-value by some more realistic and encouraging evaluation of our character. At other moments, when self-esteem is threatening to collapse into the rubble of conceit and vanity, those afflictions which eventually impair judgement and weaken relationships, a quiet word from someone who cares can restore a balanced sense of our personal short-fallings.

Because of the connecting passage between doing and being it is important to shut the door between them as firmly as possible, so that one can comment on performance without the person concerned feeling that his whole life and personality are under scrutiny. Moreover, like a medieval confessor, a manager should not offer appraisal unless he is willing to undergo appraisal himself. And he should offer his comments in such a way that he maintains, restores or enhances a person's sense of value, which is one of our most precious possessions.

People on the receiving end of praise often exhibit what seems to be embarrassment, as if they do not know how to respond. Some social psychologists, who have perhaps misunderstood the significance of value in social life, have interpreted these reactions as evidence of the manipulating nature of praise. Certainly the embarrassment may be a sign that the praised person has seen through the false motives or insincerity behind the compliments. On the other hand it may be modesty at work.

Modesty is the active way that a good person responds to praise from men. In Latin *modus* means a measure. A modest person checks the praise given against his own measure. If the praiser has made a mistake, and given him too much credit, he will politely return it to the sender by pointing out the facts. For example, he might draw attention to the contribution of other people to the meritorious actions or performance. Moreover the praiser and the praised may be operating by different measures. Thus it is a natural instinct for a modest man, who has enough self-esteem already, to deflect praise to the earth like lightning, so that it does not go to his head. And the most effective way of doing this is to share it with others. Thus a major recently awarded the George Cross for defusing bombs in Northern Ireland could say of his medal: 'They had to find some idiot on whom to hang it. It is a very high honour for quite a small number of people.'[2]

To reject praise absolutely, however, can be an immodest act. More accurately, it is false modesty. It denies the value or truth of someone else's statement, making him into a liar or a fraud. It denies the inherent social nature of our lives; that living consists of receiving gracefully as well as giving generously. It dries up one of the natural sources of strength and gratitude in society. Above all it is phoney or unreal. Except, of course, when such a rejection is the exaggerated first step of a conceited but reforming person who is trying to get his feet back on to firm ground.

CONSTRUCTIVE CRITICISM

It is not easy to receive praise gracefully in the spirit in which it was intended, remaining true to our own inner measures while being willing to adjust them to circumstances. But, by common consent, it is much harder to accept criticism, and by the same token it is therefore that much more difficult to give it well. Through experience most of us learn some common-sense rules for both giving and receiving criticism which judges work to be below the accepted or necessary standard of performance. For example, as already mentioned, most of us appreciate criticism which is followed by *constructive* suggestions on how to improve up to and beyond the required standard.

We tend to assume that criticism flows downwards, as it did when we were children. But in organizations criticism flows inwards (in the form of customer complaints), upwards and sideways – in all cases either taking the form of critically constructive suggestions or negative complaints. As 'to complain' meant originally 'to emit a mournful sound, groan, moan or grumble' I shall take it to mean feed-back – that there is some gap between expectation and performance. Where the complainant is ignorant of how the gap can be bridged a mere complaint is all that can be expected of him or her. For example, I may complain to the doctor if his medicine actually makes me worse; I cannot be expected to make a constructive criticism. In appraising the work of subordinates, however, I ought to be able to offer constructive criticism, i.e. some suggestions on how the work can be improved. If I cannot do that it is doubtful whether I have earned the right to lead, teach or manage.

The American psychologist George Weinberg has proposed some thought-provoking ground rules for easing difficult conversations. By some mergers I have reduced his twenty-two rules to seven for giving criticism and seven for receiving criticism. The comments under each rule are taken largely verbatim from Mr Weinberg's article.

Presenting the Case

1. *Offer criticisms in private if possible, and do not spread them unnecessarily.*

   Any effective criticism may sting a little. Your indifference to your colleague's comfort, displayed by a willingness to criticize him in front of others, will be taken at least as seriously as the content of what you say. In fairness to him, and yourself, wait until you are alone.

2. *Avoid long or predictable prefaces*

Avoid prefaces such as 'Listen. There's something I've wanted to tell you for a long time. It may hurt you, but...' In these matters it is best to come to the point without beating the daylights out of the proverbial bush. Nor should criticisms be invariably prefaced by positive evaluations which contain very little supplementary information, such as 'You are doing a fine job, but...' It is a mis-use of praise to use it as a sugary sweet. But of course criticism will be more readily received if you have gladly accepted the obligation to praise as well as criticize.

3. *Keep it as simple and as accurate as possible*

Try to make only one or two major criticisms at a time, rather than presenting a list of sixty complaints. Thus criticisms should not be allowed to pile up. Too many major and minor points thrown together reduce clarity and are ineffective, because no one can handle that amount of critical comment. Nor should the simple point be endlessly repeated. 'The reward for patient listening ought to be exoneration from hearing the same crime discussed again.' Exaggerations intended for emphasis, signalled by such words as 'always' and 'never', rob you of accuracy and the psychological advantages that go with it. Moreover, instead of statements such as 'You are bone idle' it may be usually more accurate to say 'You give me the impression of being lazy.' For that impression at least is an objective fact.

4. *Offer only constructive criticism of actions that can be changed*

No man, by taking thought, can add one cubit to his stature: it is therefore useless to criticize people for characteristics which they cannot change. Such 'personal remarks' should be eschewed. For all practical intents, this principle holds true for such qualities as integrity, honesty and moral courage. These can be acquired by the person concerned, but it usually takes a very long time.

5. *Don't compare the person's behaviour with that of others*

Comparisons are odious in appraisal conversations. 'No one wants to be described as inferior. Comparisons predispose others not to listen, even when the criticism or complaint is justified. Anyhow, such comparisons always miss the main point.'

6. *Don't talk about other people's motives when making a complaint or criticism*

Motives stand closer to the inner person than his actions, and to pass judgement on them can be interpreted as a censure of the whole man. Moreover actions are often multi-motivated, and it is fatally easy for an observer to draw the wrong conclusions about these hidden springs of behaviour, especially when the actor may himself be only dimly aware of why he does or does not do certain things. 'You give the listener reason to disregard your essential complaint if he concludes that your speculation about his motive is wrong. Don't confuse consequence and intention.' What matters is being able to back up your observations with some evidence or data. Thus an appraisal should never stray far from the facts. Avoid amateur psychology.

7. *After making a criticism in good faith, don't apologize for it*

'Apology will only renew your own conflict about whether you had the right to say what you did. It is asking the other person to brace you against the stress of disagreeing with him and imposes an unnecessary burden on him.' An apologetic, markedly diffident or embarrassed manner is inappropriate. Apologizing may be a symptom of lack of moral courage, except where it transpires that the facts are wrong. It is more fitting to thank the person concerned for listening to your criticism or complaint.

The Receiving End

1. *Be quiet while you are being criticized, and make it clear that you are listening*

'Whether you agree or not is an issue to be discussed later. Look directly at the person talking to you. Only thus can you convey open reception to what he is saying.' Gazing out of the window is not so convincing.

2. *Under no condition find fault with the person who has just criticized you*

'If he has made a grammatical error, for example, wait half an hour before telling him. It probably won't seem so important then.' The counter-attack of reciprocating the criticism implies that you interpret it as an insult. Or you become so busy in marshalling your own forces for the attack that you neglect to heed what is actually being said.

3. *Don't create the impression that the other person is destroying your spirit*

'Hardest to deal with are those who are belligerent at first, and who then, when cornered, act as though they were at the edge of despair. Don't be a fragile bully.'

4. *Don't jest or change the subject*

'Flippancy is considered contemptuous by many people and is hurtful to almost everyone.' Humour is a way of keeping matters in proportion, but a flippant reaction suggests that a person cannot take criticism seriously. Changing the subject is a more extreme form of taking flight from the issue. 'Use your intelligence to help articulate the objection, not to obscure it.'

5. *Don't caricature the complaint*

'If a person says you were *thoughtless*, don't ascribe to him the statement that you were *vicious* and then defend yourself against a charge he didn't make. The deliberate exaggeration of a charge against you amounts to a dismissal of the charge.'

6. *Don't imply that your critic has some ulterior, hostile motive*

'If you are asking *why* he objected, you are not dealing with his objection. The question about him should come later, if at all.'

7. *Convey to the other person that you understand his objection*

'Paraphrasing it is one good way of doing this. In effect, you are saying that the message is received and noted.'

At the end of his rules, by way of a summary, George Weinberg offered the following sound advice:

Don't let people carp at you on the pretext that they are giving you constructive criticism. I think you have the right at any time to ask for a short suspension of criticism. Refusal to grant it, or inability to tolerate it, betrays the compulsive critic. The ideal path is narrow: you must be open to criticism but not allow yourself to be tyrannized by it.[3]

As in the case of almost any set of rules we can think of legitimate and natural exceptions to the above fourteen precepts. But the onus is on the rule-breaker to be certain he is right in believing that he is some sort of special case. We are all unique but we are rarely special in that sense. George Weinberg has given us some high standards for both giving and receiving criticism, and they should serve as good guides for practice.

APPRAISING APPRAISALS

Sometimes there may be a negative reaction against a justified criticism, even a rejection of it. Later, however, an observer might see that the person concerned is actually working in a different and improved way. Consciously the criticism and the 'critic' have been rejected; unconsciously, or in the depth mind, the message has been hoisted in, and transformed into action. In such instances the appraiser will receive no credit, no 'reward' of gratitude from the other person. But leadership does not entitle one to such rewards. Anyway the proportion of those people who are likely to return thanks for such personal help is probably no more than about one in ten.

It may be useful to the appraiser to recall that he is addressing a person's depth mind through the gateways of the senses. And it sometimes takes time for the penny to drop, as we say. A second or third interview or conversation may become necessary, for repetition on different occasions couched in other words and images, may implant a message more firmly. Yet the balance is fine. We have to guard always 'the sacred right of rejection.' If this happens, then the appraiser has to re-appraise his advice. There are more ways than one to skin a rabbit, and it may be possible to accept the difference of opinion bravely. On the other hand, the person's prospects or even very employment may rest upon their acceptance of the proposed improvement. If this is so, it is of course essential that it is made absolutely clear during the interview.

Conclusion

Appraising is the difficult art of communicating your evaluation of another person's work and conduct to him in a face-to-face conversation or interview. It is vital to choose the right words and phrases to express your reactions in a simple, clear and lively way. As a general rule, appraisal should focus upon what a person has done or not done in terms of their observable effects upon the common task, team maintenance and the needs of other individuals. It should not invade the inner world of motives and values or the more-or-less fixed sphere of temperament or disposition. Comment in the latter areas, if invited or deemed necessary for some reason, should be properly prefaced by a suitable and sincere diffidence, such as 'It seems to me...' or 'You give me the impression of...' All observations should be supported by some data, which has been naturally acquired, i.e. without opening yourself to the charge that you have been spying, encouraging informers or snooping.

Communication is a two-way affair, and it is essential for the communicant to be confident that he drinks in merited praise without letting it go to his head, finding in it confirmation of what he stands for and the endeavour of his life, and also storing from it encouragement for the dark days ahead, as in stone cisterns. Under criticism, the truth of which he recognizes, the communicant should work with his critic to identify the area for improvement, like a fellow surgeon working around an operating table. What should matter to both of them is the improvement in common work. Nor will he be distracted by imperfections in his appointed (or self-appointed) critic: truth is truth whether it comes from the mouths of angels or fish-wives. To receive criticism well and to act upon it is the ultimate badge of the good listener. If it is unjustified, as later certified by completely impartial 'appeal judges', still the appraisal interview can be creatively turned into an occasion for learning humility.

From the leader's point of view, the power of his praises and criticisms will stand in proportion to the respect he has aroused. At their heights his evaluations can approach the blessings and curses of the Biblical prophets in their power to enhance values or to destroy confidence and even life. The good leader uses his power of praising or criticizing judiciously to achieve good purposes, while building up the community and forwarding the growth of individuals. With regard to the latter, he might well meditate occasionally on the prayer of the psalmist: 'Let the righteous rather smite me friendly: and reprove me. But let not their precious balms break my head.'[4]

This consideration of the opportunities and difficulties of giving and receiving of both praise and criticism leads us back to the centrality of integrity, both in its professional and personal senses. Integrity is the quality which makes people trust one another. As Peter Drucker has finely concluded in perhaps the most widely-read book on management in the Western world:

> When all is said and done, developing men still requires a basic quality in the manager which cannot be created by supplying skills or by emphasizing the importance of the task. It requires integrity of character... It may be argued that every occupation — the doctor, the lawyer, the grocer — requires integrity. But there is a difference. The manager lives with the people he manages, he decides what their work is to be, he directs it, he trains them for it, he appraises it and, often, he decides their future. The relationship of merchant and client requires honourable dealings. Being a manager, though, is

more like being a parent, or a teacher. And in these relationships honourable dealings are not enough; personal integrity is of the essence.[5]

CHAPTER ELEVEN

COURSES: TRAINING FOR COMMUNICATION

What I hear, I forget; what I see, I remember,
What I do, I know

ANON.

Many organizations and professions include or make available training in some or all of the facets of communication described in this book. Such skills as Public Speaking, Effective Writing and Faster Reading, for example, appear often in their programmes. In other parts of their programmes, especially in higher educational centres, business schools, universities and polytechnics, students inquire into the nature of organizations, studying the tributary disciplines of psychology, social psychology and sociology. But attempts at integrating these studies are rare. Nor is there record of any thorough research into the teaching of communication, although many hail it as one of the more important items on the management education agenda.

While claiming no particular originality for its content or methods I shall set out one possible shape such an integrated course might take. The educational and training needs of organizations are so varied that few of them would wish to take any course 'off the peg'. Therefore this outline programme is offered essentially as a set of guidelines and not a blueprint. Consequently the principles behind it matter more than the details, for principles – once grasped – can be applied flexibly while the rigid adherence to someone else's design deadens all concerned. The fundamental factors involved are considered under the six headings of the Communication Star.

AIM

In working organizations any aim or objective has to be ultimately justifiable as instrumental to the over-all purpose, hence the importance of thinking out the latter as clearly as possible and communicating it. Granted the relevance of good communication to that purpose, the first action must be to define the aim. It is possible to spend far too much time on the wording of what must inevitably be a fairly general statement, especially if the course does attempt to draw the threads together and bind them into a strong rope.

Besides emphasizing the work-centred nature of the course (thus distinguishing it from the esoteric, artistic or mechanical possibilities conjured up by the word 'communication') the aim should also reflect the fact that the responsibility for the outcome of the course is shared with the course members. Lastly, it needs to be short and concise.

These characteristics are only possible if the aim is immediately refracted into more tangible or concrete objectives, each compassing one phase or part of the course. On a trial-run course for 'middle managers', of Whitbreads Ltd., the aim and objectives were defined as follows:

The AIM of the Course is to give each course member the opportunity to develop his effectiveness in the field of communication.

The more specific OBJECTIVES for each participant are:-

— to deepen awareness of the need for good communication at all levels;
— to give an understanding of the nature and principles of communication;
— to develop an appreciation of the necessary organizational structure and atmosphere for effective communication;
— to provide exercises for the practice of the essential skills of communication;
— to improve effective communication in his own area of responsibility.

COURSE MEMBERS

Who should come on an integrated Communication Course? From all the evidence it is clear that almost everyone working with other people would benefit from such a course, providing it was properly planned. For, as in the case of all the really important and interesting subjects, nobody can ever say that they have 'done' communication: there is always more to be learnt. The priority groups are obviously trainees and junior managers; the younger the better. Once, at the age of 15 years, I attended an Army one-day 'Methods of Instruction' course and it still stands out in my memory as a strikingly interesting, practical and enjoyable day. Indeed it has always made me doubt those who doubt the value of short courses or programmes.

Whatever their age or background, course members should be thoroughly briefed on the aims and objectives of the course, and why they have been chosen for it. They should have a personal objective for attending. Pre-course questionnaires can also be useful means for increasing knowledge about the course members — their needs and expectations as far as communication is concerned. For example, the first question on one pre-course questionnaire — 'What are the main weaknesses as far as communication is concerned in industry from your own experience?' — produced the following crop of answers:

Thoughtless action without reasonable consultation. Information communicated down, not always passed to all line management.

The absence of a continuing briefing on Company Policy from Senior Management to all levels of Employees.

Communication (lateral) between departments. Lack of comparative knowledge of how other allied companies work.

Communication to shop floor poor with points not fully understood.

Communications are frequently distorted at all levels by the communicators allowing their personalities to protrude into the communication.

Tendency to delay in communication decisions.

The written word is often confused with unnecessary jargon, complicating many simple statements both written and oral.

Too many grape-vines.

'Them and Us' i.e. natural reluctance to agree with the other side, even if logically they wish to.

There is not sufficient consideration given to the phrase 'who needs to know?'

Often a lack of desire to communicate.

When there is a desire to communicate:-

(i)   seldom time to do a good job.
(ii)   often difficulties because of length of lines of communication.

Insufficient feed-back from the shop floor upwards.

The grape-vine is usually first, and indeed often supplies information that is never provided through the 'proper' channels. Information that is effectively transmitted still tends to be what it is thought people ought to know and not what they really want to know.

To some extent these comments highlight some of the weaknesses in communication in all large organizations. Moreover, they serve to underline the importance of getting to know as early as possible the considerable knowledge about communication which the course members have already gained from their experience in organizations and will be bringing with them to the course.

THE CONTENT

The possible contents for a short integrated course on communication for managers have been covered in the preceding chapters. However short the course, communication deserves to be presented as a whole. In other words, all the contents sign-posted by the chapter headings in this book merit at least some attention. The *level* of this attention will naturally depend upon the other factors in the Communication Star. Nor should all the subjects necessarily receive the same level of treatment. For example, on the specimen course I shall describe some topics obviously receive more weight than others, reflecting the special needs of the Whitbread Group.

In any integrated training course the advantages of doing it in a concentrated form — rather than spreading it in penny packets over a long period of time — outweigh the disadvantages. It takes time to stir up the maximum interest and involvement at the start of a course, and then time at the end to relate the general ideas and experience culled from research or other work settings to the particular needs of the course members and their particular oganization. Time is also required for digestion without distraction. Possibly the ideal length would be a short concentrated course of from three to five days, with some follow-up sessions (perhaps half-days) from time to time.

Some readers may judge this to be short time for such an

all-embracing subject. It should be emphasized, however, that the course only covers the *content* of communication. The *practice* of communication is best done in relation with other activities or studies. For communication is primarily a means to other ends. The more the practice of it can be realistic in that it involves real intentions and real contents the more students will learn from it. At Sandhurst, for example, it was possible to introduce military history presentations to give each officer cadet the opportunity for practising his speaking skills. But such practice needs to be discussed in the light of a common 'model' of communication, sets of principles and target skills. The trainers, be they academics, officers or managers, have to be themselves skilled in the art of getting two crops from ground where only one grew before.

The content, then, of an integrated course might include:

The Nature of Communication (non-verbal; role of language; dialogue; the Communication Star).

The Four Basic Skills:

SPEAKING: (The Search for Rules; Five Principles — Be Prepared Clear, Simple, Vivid and Natural; Audio-Visual Aids)

LISTENING: (Ten Symptoms of Poor Listening; Five Steps to Better Listening; Trust)

WRITING: (Style; Better Usage; Word Power; Phrases; Letters; Reports)

READING: (Reading Speeds; Perusing; Five Guidelines for Reading; Building a Library)

Communication in Organizations (Size; Models — Network, System and Body; Trefoil Model of Needs; Priorities; Methods: Line Management, Briefing Groups, Joint Consultations, Committees, House Journals and Surveys, Industrial Relations and Grape-vines; Corporate Integrity)

Leadership of Meetings (Kinds of Meeting; Leadership Functions: Initiating, Planning, Controlling, Supporting, Informing and Evaluating; Conference Leadership; Leadership Manner)

Appraising Performance (The Effects of Praise, Constructive Criticism, Presenting the Case — Seven Points; The Receiving End — Seven Points)

Of course this list of contents is not exhaustive. For example, it may be judged desirable to expand it to include more sessions on interviewing, tele-communications or faster reading. Some topics, on the other hand, may be covered in other courses, and it may be sufficient for the tutor to make the link explicit and leave it at that. But the above programme, it may be claimed, does cover those core elements in communication which can be studied at the adult level with interest and profit.

PROGRAMME DESIGN

A course on communication in organizations ought to go through the following main phases. First, it needs an introductory session which covers the aim and objectives of the course, delves into the reasons why they are worth-while and exposes some of the practical problems of communication present in the experience of the members. Secondly the general nature of the subject, using a model such as the Communication Star, should be explored. The four basic skills come next in logical order as the third phase, possibly accompanied by a session on non-verbal communication. The fourth phase might consider the organizational aspects, leading on to practice sessions in chairing meetings and conducting meetings. The last phase ought to revolve around the application of the course to each individual's working situation.

In the realities of busy life it may not be possible to adhere to even this general order, let alone a blueprint. Moreover, in a longer than three-days' course, the principle of variety argues for a mixture of different kinds of session and focus. But it is useful to bear in mind when designing a particular course the simple progression: General Skills; Organization — Small Groups — Face-to-Face; Applications. Over-lapping or inversions prove acceptable providing the wholeness of the course is explained in advance, and the individual parts related to some sort of sketch-map model.

METHODS

The methods chosen should be such that they contribute substantially to the achievement of the aim. The Whitbread Course Aim, for example, suggests the employment of methods which give the course members maximum opportunity to *participate* in the training. It places the tutor or trainer more in a supporting and guiding role. But that aim also requires a certain carefully judged 'input' of ideas and information.

Besides serving the aim the methods used should reflect the nature of the content. For example, in a course which emphasized the importance of *dialogue* in communication it would be disappointing to find a heavy reliance on the monologue method of the lecture. In a programme which preached the value of feedback you would hope to see some kind of feedback or evaluation being positively encouraged and planned for by the course leaders. For this reason such methods as visual aids or films have to be of the highest quality, otherwise they will strike a note of disharmony with the content of the course.

The methods should also show respect for the status, knowledge and experience of the communicants or course members. The most obvious manifestation of this respect is the willingness of the course tutor to listen and learn himself. This interest must, of course, be genuine or unfeigned: the test of it is the trainer's readiness to do things differently or to change his own views if convinced. As he must also hold certain concepts and approaches which he is offering firmly and enthusiastically, not from the book but because he believes them to be true, such flexibility is not always easy or common. Unless he can practise and convey it, however, the tutor is not teaching communication, he is talking *about* communication.

Working in Small Groups

These considerations taken together place a premium first on methods which allow full *participation*. The value of small discussion groups for the promotion of thinking, discovery and action has been well established. People learn more readily by comparing notes with each other rather than with the tutor viewed as an outside source of infallible but irrelevant pronouncements. It does not help much for the teacher merely to deny that he possesses any special authority, and then to keep on talking. For it is the *pattern* of such communication which is wrong, not necessarily the content.

The break from the centrality of monologue leads to the small group of 5—8 people as the focus of the methods. The actual number depends on a variety of factors, notably time. The numbers must be small enough to allow each person to think aloud and engage in conversation with the others fully if he wants to do so. Yet the numbers must be large enough to make the exchange of views interesting and novel to the end. The length of the course is a factor in the last calculation. The longer it is the more people it should include.

In a two- or three-day course these factors suggest a course membership of 15, 18, 20 or 21, doing most of their work in small groups of 5, 6 or 7 members. Allowing for one inter-change of small-group membership during the course, seven is the maximum number for the small group. The difference between 7 and 9 is very marked in that the latter figure allows one or two of the more diffident to be more-or-less left out of the discussion. Three syndicates or small groups give a better cross section of views than two; they promote more thought while at the same time preventing any polarization of 'us' and 'them', which is a latent possibility in the two-syndicate approach. Moreover, a course membership of more than 21 makes plenary discussion difficult to sustain. The Whitbread Course of 18 members, working in three groups, seemed right for a duration of four-and-a-half days.

The method of making the small group or syndicate work *precede* rather than follow the plenary session is advocated here. The advantages of this approach are that it promotes thought and creates a high quality of listening. Its supposed disadvantage, that the members will not have enough to talk about without hearing a lecture or talk first, clearly does not apply in the field of communication studies with adults.

The group methods described briefly above develop such a sense of participation and involvement that many teachers have now become 'group centred' in their training assumptions. But other general methods have an important place alongside – and complementary to – small-group and plenary discussion: the lecture, film and film-strips, case studies and projects.

Lecture, as a word, has some unfortunate overtones. It conjures up an hour-long monologue, delivered in some academic setting. Moreover its origins suggest the activity of reading out aloud a prepared discourse, a form of public speaking which now strikes us as archaic. Therefore it is not surprising that the lecture has fallen into disrepute among all except the die-hards. For the reasons noted above there are good grounds for this diminishing enthusiasm, but – like many reactions – it can go too far.

All too often the present-day substitutes for the lecture – variously called theory presentations, addresses or talks – over-react by being short, ill-prepared, without order, spoilt by interruptions; they appear casual and slovenly, being illustrated only by some indecipherable scribblings on large sheets of newsprint with crayons. In other words, lectures have not been abolished, but replaced by a bad form of lecturing. Obviously we cannot employ the traditional university lecture as the main method of instruction in the training field: the evidence is overwhelmingly against it. But training and education merge into each other in the organizational and human fields, and the lecture method in its essence, i.e. one person expounding a subject for a certain length of time, has certain irreplaceable contributions to make to the learning experience. Thus the option is not 'to lecture or not to lecture', but between giving good or bad lectures (See Appendix 3).

Within the context of a course on communication it is especially important that lectures should be good in terms of both content and the use of methods such as visual aids. In a long course there is room for one or two talks or lectures on tangential subjects, such as 'Communication in the Theatre' or 'Tele-Communications' or 'Advertising'. But these should be seen as the cream on the top, not the bread, butter or jam themselves. It should be possible to capture something of the ideal drawn by L. S. Powell even in a 'lecturette' or talk of twenty minutes or less in the sessions of the main-stream syllabus on communication in working life.

Films

Like lectures, films may be divided into those which are geared to play a part in training sessions along with discussions, demonstrations and practice, and those which were made for entertainment but have some relevance.

In the first category there is a general shortage of good management-training films. With regard to communication I have found the following to be valuable:

Talkback (18 minutes. Black-and-white. Rank)

This film is shot in an industrial setting, using the flashback method as a management consultant recalls particular incidents on a recent assignment. The film illustrates the effects of different 'frames of reference' over the meanings of words and phrases such as 'economic use of materials'; seeing things through departmental blinkers; lack of feedback; and the breakdown in genuine dialogue. The excellent handbook which accompanies the film shows how it can be stopped after each 'phase' for discussion and comment. It also mentions briefing groups and noticeboards.

Talkback is an example of the better films available for management education. Many of the others are either poor in quality (being filmed lectures), or dated, or geared too exclusively to the level of the junior entrant into organizational life. On the Whitbreads course, however, we used *Letter Writing at Work* (UK, Rank, 19 minutes), *Visual Aids* (UK, Ministry of Defence (Navy), 27 minutes) and *Are You Listening?* (USA, Henry Strauss Productions, 10 minutes). The last two, along with some thirty other films grouped under the heading of 'Communications', are discussed in:

Films for Managers: A Guide to Management and Supervisory Training Films Available in the United Kingdom, edited by Marilyn J. Jacobs (Management Publications Limited, revised edition 1971). This book gives reviews or synopses of each film listed, together with details of running time, distributor, hire or purchase price, year of release and other relevant information. It also includes some valuable hints on using film in the training context.

Film Strips

The obvious advantage of film strips is that they allow discussion more readily than films; they are also cheaper and more easy to show in many situations. On its two-day Supervisory Training Course for the Bank of England, for example, the Industrial Society has made use of the following filmstrips (all obtainable from it on hire or purchase):

> *Introducing Changes*
> *Can You State a Case?*
> *Can You Conduct an Interview?*
> *How do You Instruct?*

Personally, however, I find filmstrips rather slow and static for the kind of fast-moving and participatory training which I advocate at middle- or senior-management levels, but they are perhaps especially adapted to the supervisory and junior-management levels of training.

Case Studies and Exercises.

The case study method fits in easily with the participatory methods of working. On the second Whitbread course, as a result of a desire expressed by members on the first, I included a case study session on the Charge of the Light Brigade (see Chapter Two). The members were given it on the evening prior to the course, and tackled it in syndicates on the first day, immediately after the session on 'The Nature of Communication'. There were asked the following questions:

1. Please identify the six points of the Communication Star in this episode.

2. Why did communication fail?
3. How would you have ensured successful communication?

In the sessions on organizations and briefing groups there is also room for short case studies. Some sources for suitable case study material are given at the end of this chapter. For such topics as the leadership of meetings or appraising performance, practical exercises are more appropriate than case studies. In the context of longer courses more elaborate exercises in communication are possible, simulating the flow of ideas and information between departments in large organizations, but these take up too much time on short courses. References to two articles by Dr. P. Hesseling (of the Technical Efficiency Department, Philips NV, Holland), describing such longer exercises, are given later.

Individual Projects
The contemporary emphasis in training and group work can sometimes lead to an obscuring of the importance of the individual. It is the development of the individual *in* groups and organizations that matters. To some extent he or she can be developed by the group or organization, but perhaps to a more limited measure than current orthodoxy believes. Nor is the individual to be 'developed' solely *for* the group or organization as some practitioners seem to believe. For an individual person is always an end as well as a means. Although all management, professional or industrial training must regard him mainly as an instrument, albeit one who has freely consented to be used for the corporate purpose, yet the complementary sense of the individual as an end in himself (which should predominate in the school, college and university) needs to be there in the background. For there is a real sense in which the group and organization exist to promote effective individuals.

In a short course of three days or less it is difficult to include much individual private or guided study. But speaking and writing lend themselves naturally to individual practice. In a course of three to five days, each course member should be able to give a short prepared talk and also to tackle some 'Better Writing' assignments. If two tutors are engaged with eighteen course members an individual critique for the written piece, be it a letter, precis or report, should be possible. The individual tutorial, however, although immensely valuable, does eat into the tutor's time.

The project has the advantage of promoting individual study and learning during the course, before it or after it. As a schoolboy I tackled a history project, and in the 1960s I introduced the method into the teaching of military history at Sandhurst. The holistic nature of a project, the shared decision on its contents, the freedom over timetables: all these factors make it absorbing for a student providing that the teacher is interested and competent as a guide. It is quite possible that project work calls upon different orders of ability than examinations. Certainly whether done by individuals or by small teams, as in 'presentations', the project method is a powerful learning strategy.

As the report *Education for Management: A Study of Resources* (HMSO, 1972) reveals, over half the teachers in this field use project methods customarily and another quarter use them occasionally. But it points out that further inquiry is badly needed into the various activities to which the name is applied and what circumstances are necessary for them to be effective learning situations. Thus it is important at this stage to describe exactly how the project method can be used in communication training.

In Whitbread the projects followed on after the course. The objective, method and desired results of each was discussed and decided on during the week; six months later the findings on each were presented to a reconvened course at a day-long session. The time constraints and the more limited aim and objectives of a communication course favour this latter approach. Before the course, however, the Whitbread members did have their ten-minute talks to prepare, besides a fairly lengthy pre-course questionnaire to complete.

Projects are demanding not only in time but also in knowledge, for the tutor must be able to offer guidance and encouragement over a wide range of possible themes or variations on them. But the rewards in terms of the natural motivation of the individual and the sense of shared discovery are such that they ensure a promising future for the project method at all levels of training and education.

THE SITUATION
From the preceding sections it is deducible that the setting for a communication course needs a room large enough for the 18–24 members to sit at 'horse-shoe' tables, with points for film and slide projection, overhead projector and tape-recorders. At least one of the three or four syndicate rooms needs to be large enough to take half the course when it divides into two for speaking practice. These are the essentials. The setting should also be free from unnecessary distractions, which is an argument for holding the course away from the works

environment. The alternative is to make an island of the training centre or department and guard the course jealously from the long arm of unnecessary telephone interruptions.

THE COMMUNICATORS

It would be rare indeed to find one person omni-competent in all the aspects of communication to be included on the course. Even if he could be found it would offend against the principle of variety to have him hold forth for more than three days. On a two- or three-day course there are big advantages in having two tutors involved. One of them should be responsible for integrating the course as its leader, but the other could play a major part as co-leader by administrative support and by taking some of the sessions.

In large organizations or longer courses the staff should become a team of specialists, who work together under the leader, like musicians working from a common score and under a single conductor. For example, the four basic skills lend themselves to specialist parts. In the case of the Whitbread Course of four-and-a-half days, besides two Whitbread staff training managers and myself, three members of the Industrial Society tackled half-day sessions on Writing, Meetings and Briefing Groups respectively. It was found that a half-day's briefing before the course was essential in order to weld a unity of approach while accommodating the natural and desirable individual preferences for particular aspects or selections within their chosen areas.

Granted the enthusiasm and general teaching ability of the course staff there still remains the problem of 'training the trainers' in this particular and demanding field of applied study. It is doubtful whether books, even those more text-bookish than this one, can do the trick on their own. Books do not communicate to that extent. Trainers need demonstration, practice under an experienced eye, experiment on their own, discussion and then reading last of all. At best a book may inspire them to have a go. Therefore it is to be hoped that some national body with the public interest at heart will take up the challenge and provide such a 'training for trainers' that takes into account not only the shades of theory and ranges of methods involved, but also the greater professionalism and higher expectations of training managers, educators and teachers in their respective spheres.

Like many other subjects, however, communication is too important to be left entirely to the specialists. The advantages of involving 'line managers' in training are manifest anyway, and communication courses are no exception. The presence of the Archbishops of York and

Canterbury on successive Windsor courses, of the Managing Director and other Directors on the Whitbread courses and various Generals and even one Secretary of State for War at Sandhurst presentations, to go back further in time: all these have made a powerful impact on the quality of learning and its relevance to everyday life. Communication courses, in short, should not be merely about communication: they should include unusual and striking examples of real communication through dialogue.

EVALUATION

Like all training in the related areas of 'the human side of enterprise' there is no single quantifiable yardstick of evaluation. Therefore the trainer (and organization) must rely on four or five imperfect measures as the basis for a holistic or growing single judgement. Such a judgement must be grounded in some kind of objective data, which will include the trainer's own subjective feelings. The distinction between objective and subjective is useful, but like all such distinctions it cannot be maintained rigidly. Judgement by its nature implies both.

Such imperfect measures as (1) course member's written reactions, (2) post-course reactions (3) observed improvements by bosses, (4) financial effects of projects, (5) opinions of experienced practitioners – all have a contribution to make. To some extent numbers can be put upon them, for some people do find it possible to place their reactions on a simple scale, be it 1–9 or 1–100. Written comments, however, do reveal more than numbers.

There are good reasons for treating with caution course reaction sheets, even anonymous ones. Participation and involvement do lead to enjoyment and a profitable exchange of views, and the end-of-course euphoria, coupled with a desire to be generous, can result in a spate of pleasant remarks. But cynical dismissal of this method of evaluation is not justified. Providing that participants are asked searching questions and it is made clear that honest answers are expected, they are still a most useful source of evaluation.

Conclusion

In the past, training given under the heading of 'Communication' has been partial in scope – confining itself to techniques and skills rather than the art of Communication in organizations. But all these aspects are inter-related and inter-dependent. The time has come for us to look upon good communication as a whole, depending upon factors in the organization, groups and individuals. To concentrate on any one of the factors to the exclusion of the others is to miss the point.

Training for communication is perfectly possible. Providing the six elements in the Communication Star are got right the course will be a success. Still more, the success will be consolidated if the training is followed up soon by better training on the job by a course member's own leader who has himself been through a similar course. In this chapter the requirements under those six headings have been discussed.

So much for the aerodynamics of the course. The actual design of the 'aeroplane' must be left to each organization in the light of its particular circumstances, although some ready-made or all-purpose models, based on logical sequence, would be useful for the busy training manager. Also some discussion and practice in the arts of piloting such a course — getting it off the ground, monitoring the dials and landing it — would not be out of place. All these, it is hoped, will come soon.

In the meantime the many organizations already doing some training in the field of communication might fruitfully pause and take stock. Are there any vital ingredients which they are virtually ignoring? Are they using up-to-date methods? Such technological innovations as closed-circuit television or overhead projectors can often disguise lack of progress in the human methods described above, notably the use of small groups in structured training courses.

Thus for organizations, working groups and individuals the importance of good communication grows daily in proportion with the problems and obstacles which make it so difficult. The weeds grow fast and profusely, and it takes dedication, effort and skill to keep the life-line canals open and bearing the right two-way traffic. Behind good communication lies the cardinal necessity for creative education and effective training.

CHAPTER TWELVE

ACTION PROGRAME: HOW TO IMPROVE
YOUR COMMUNICATION

Personally I am always ready to learn,
although I do not always like to be taught.
SIR WINSTON CHURCHILL

The preceding chapters may well have achieved their objectives and developed in you the reader both a greater awareness of the elements in communication, and an increased understanding of the art which blends them into ever-new patterns and harmonies. But it is by practice or *doing* that we learn most, and, as the end of this book is near, you may now wish to begin to formulate your own plan for improving communication.

As a preliminary it is helpful to diagnose as accurately as possible the areas in which you would like those improvements to take place. Communication is such an all-embracing subject that it is easy to be too general about it. Some limitation or narrowing of focus is necessary. Therefore it is suggested that you should set your sights on some few limited objectives, attainable in the next three months or so, and not frame altruistic New Year's resolutions, or seek to reform the entire organization in which you work (unless you happen to be a chairman or managing director).

Once you have identified your own training needs (with or without some friendly help), mark the chapters or pages in this book which deserve to be re-read in the light of them. Then read them extra-critically, adding your own notes or observations if necessary, so that the conclusions become your own. At this point scan ahead in your timetable to see if there is an occasion, time or opportunity which naturally suggests itself for practical experiment. For example, your diary may tell you that on such-and-such a date you must give a talk to a group, or chair a meeting: golden opportunities for applying some lessons. Or a forthcoming holiday may be the time for following up some of the ideas and suggestions on reading in Chapter Eight.

Having written down your own programme of not more than, say, five points – each with time limits – the next step is to mark down a day for a progress review. Again this appointment with yourself (and this book) can best be made firm by writing it in your diary in red ink. So that in about three months time you have fixed to review your own Five-Point Programme against your conclusions or decisions stemming from your reading of the above chapters.

During this exercise in 'self-management by objectives' (as we could call it) it is important to inoculate yourself in advance against discouragement. We suffer from forgetful minds, and our reach always exceeds our grasp. At the end of three months you may only have discovered just how unaware you are of the dimension of communication, how little you understand the other points in the Communication Star (other than yourself) and how noticeably you lack some or all of the skills which others exercise so gracefully. As teachers know so well, that will be your crucial moment. Either you give up the struggle or you resolve to go on come what may. Blame this book, curse your lack of time, wait for an easier method: these are useful alibis for those who choose the former course. But, if you embrace the second one, you will have gained from the 'self-management by objectives' exercise a far more valuable weapon than any technique: a much greater willingness to go on practising and learning even although you now realize — with humility — that it will take a lifetime to make much progress.

You may already have decided long ago upon such a lifelong strategy, in which case this book may only suggest some more tactical moves. Or you may be embarking on the enterprise of seeking to master the art of communication, not without a sense of excitement or freshly rekindled interest. In the latter cases it may be helpful to set down alongside your own 'action programme' a more general strategy which can be the source of new ideas for later programmes. Such a strategy can also act as a framework, reminding you of the unfinished business on the agenda, even when you have honestly won gains in one or two of the areas of your choice. The following ten suggestions may serve as such a guide. They should not be regarded as infallible, but simply as ways of translating the message of the Communication Star into a form so that you can use them yourself. In writing them I have followed the excellent headings of the 'Ten Commandments for Good Communication', published by the American Management Association, but I have re-worded the comments underneath them and added some observations and suggestions of my own.

1 SEEK TO CLARIFY YOUR IDEAS BEFORE COMMUNICATING

The more thoroughly we analyse the problem or idea, the clearer it should become. This search for preliminary clarity is the first step toward any effective communication. In the terms of the Communication Star it concerns above all the *content* element. Only as a result of a considerable amount of thinking (and sometimes hard wrestling with problems) does the content yield up its treasures of clarity, simplicity and vividness.

In this respect communication is often faulty because it is like a house built on weak foundations. The remedy is to check mentally each communication to see whether or not it is as clear and as simple as possible. If it can be colourful as well, that is an extra bonus. If it still seems unduly complicated or vague, then the matter may not yet be ready for communication. Thought should dispel these opaque and diffuse facets, so that the matter becomes crystal clear and reveals its natural order.

2 EXAMINE THE TRUE PURPOSE OF EACH COMMUNICATION

Ask yourself always what you want really to accomplish with your message. It may be to initiate action, to win commitment, to enlarge understanding or to change attitudes. Once you have identified the most important target – the MUST bull on the target opposed to the SHOULD and COULD inner and outer rings – then your plan, language and tone should reflect that goal. The art of communication lies not least in the ability to fashion means to fit ends neatly and appropriately. But this message implies the prior activity of defining the objective as precisely as possible. It is a common mistake to attempt too much in any one communication. The sharper the focus of the intention the greater its chances of being realized.

3 CONSIDER THE TOTAL PHYSICAL AND HUMAN SETTING WHENEVER YOU COMMUNICATE

This guide-line embraces two other key elements in the Communication Star: the recipients and the situation. The receivers or communicants bring their own past history, education, frames of reference, meanings and expectations to the communication. It is a sign of a good communicator (to repeat the point) if he spends as much time on understanding people as he does grasping his subject.

Also the communicator can fruitfully develop a greater sensitivity to the total physical and human situation which forms the context of the actual or proposed communication. The situation is simply the particular combination of circumstances. Most situations share some general features in common, otherwise it would be pointless to frame any rules at all. It is very rare for us to find ourselves in a situation without any kind of parallel in human experience or history. But conversely all situations have certain particular features, their unique aspect.

From the standpoint of a communicator it is important to check your sense of *timing* against the situation. The circumstances in which you make an announcement or ask a question will affect its outcome. As the old saying puts it, there is a time and place for everything. If waiting is often included in the strategy of a good communicator then timing is part of his tactics. To a large extent timing is a natural talent, like an ear for music. But it can be developed by a constant attention to the actual situation — its present weather or mood, hopes and fears, as well as the more permanent attitudes and values which sustain it.

The principle that the situation influences the relationships of people (and therefore communication), and is conversely controlled and modified by them, reaches down to the *physical* environment too. Should you communicate in private, for example, or otherwise? Improving the physical conditions for a communication can contribute considerably to its outcome.

Within an organization this principle includes understanding thoroughly the total communication system, the sum of all the methods outlined in Chapter Four and how they inter-act with each other in a living way. So that we know instinctively in a given situation what are the appropriate channels for sending messages upwards, downwards or sideways. Thus we avoid the twin errors of communicating to too few on the one hand and too many on the other.

4 CONSULT WITH OTHERS, WHERE APPROPRIATE, IN PLANNING COMMUNICATION

One of the best and simplest ways of improving the methods you employ in communication is to discuss them and even try them out with others first. These discussions, trial runs or rehearsals may additionally throw up questions about the aim and the content, but they are especially valuable for exposing the drawbacks or weaknesses of the method employed.

As a principle, the sooner that others are involved in planning a communication the better. If it is left until the eleventh hour the form of the communication (including the audio-visual aids) may have so 'hardened' in the communicator's mind that he will be reluctant to make substantial changes. Or it may be literally too late. Far better, present your tentative draft and sketches first, and then have one or two more rehearsals later. Even if it is only a matter of asking a question or making a complaint it is a good self-training practice, if time allows, to check the wording with someone else. Wives, colleagues and secretaries will often agree to act as consultants in this way before a communication takes its final shape.

5 BE MINDFUL, WHILE YOU COMMUNICATE, OF THE OVER-TONES AS WELL AS THE BASIC CONTENT OF YOUR MESSAGE

All that we can do over our non-verbal communication is to be aware that it is going out from us all the time, like radio waves which the communicant can pick up. Then we can endeavour to tune these transmissions into the intentions of minds and hearts. In practice this means eliminating or controlling the distractors, such as mannerisms. Also it entails allowing the natural tone of voice, facial expression and gesture to integrate freely into the message.

This awareness or sensitivity should extend to language as well. The emotional overtones of some words are well known: they have the power (because we give it them) to conjure up the feelings they signify. A 'trigger' word or phrase can explode like a detonator in another person's mind. All words have their attendant aura tails, like stars or tadpoles. A sense of these shades of meaning can be easily developed by turning often to a fat and well-fed dictionary. Such a habit also aids clarity.

There is also the possibility that whatever is strongly in your personality, but not necessarily expressed in word or outward sign, will be picked up by the other person. People who are not themselves very articulate can be experts at sensing what is in your mind, just as babies seem to pick up their mothers' emotions. Fear is especially contagious, as are all the negative attitudes or emotions, such as hostility or embarrassment. Most of us recognize the presence of these feelings by physical sensations of tenseness, heart beating or going hot-and-cold. Conversely, we may feel warm, stimulated or better — we know not why. It is important for the communicator to sense when the atmosphere is charged in this way, and to be aware that his own total communication is flowing into it, like a river into a sea. To some extent, we can practise changing the atmosphere by selecting our own attitudes more carefully.

175

6 TAKE THE OPPORTUNITY, WHEN IT ARISES, TO CONVEY SOMETHING OF HELP OR VALUE TO THE RECEIVER

It is easy (but fatal in the long-term) to reduce this guide to a formalized and insincere ritual of 'praise first, then criticize'. A few sugary phrases of flattery before the 'But' ... which starts the real point of the meeting: all too often appraisals take this unimaginative form. Yet communication depends on the strength of the line of relationship between two or more people. And the way to build up that relationship is by using it frequently to convey helpful or valuable ideas or information, so that the positive attitude behind all good communication becomes manifested.

This practice stems best from the habitual attitude of 'doing unto others as we would have them do unto us'. We like to receive helpful suggestions, or communications which enhance our own sense of the worth-whileness of our contributions. If we have made some kind of special effort we appreciate the finishing touch of a genuine 'thank-you' from those who have benefited. Yet we are often slow to take up our daily opportunities for giving help, bringing something valuable to or showing a lively concern for another person or persons.

It is true that communicants will be more willing to receive criticism or ill-tidings from a person whom they have grown to trust through the tenor of his general communication with them. But if they detect that this positive communication is developed only with ulterior motives in mind, the results will be disastrous. Eventually want of sincerity breeds want of trust. In a faithless atmosphere even offers of help, gifts and compliments will be greeted with suspicion and perhaps fear. If we entertain positive attitudes towards people it is natural for us to want to bring them good news or constructive help whenever we can, simply because we like them.

7 FOLLOW UP YOUR COMMUNICATION

We shall not be able to improve our communication unless we find out how effective it has been. You can actively follow up some communications by encouraging feedback from the receiver through asking questions and by a positive attitude to any opinions he may offer. But should you rely upon the immediate verbal feedback? Try asking the same questions some days or weeks after the communication.

Another useful yardstick is to review behaviour or performance. If the original communication aimed at some change in the way someone does something, look over the heads of their initial reaction — positive or negative — and see what actually has changed. If nothing has happened the temptation is to blame the people concerned. But the communicator should first reassess his own communication to diagnose more precisely why it has failed. Did you really make clear enough the changes that were required? Did you check sufficiently thoroughly that everyone understood his part?

8 COMMUNICATE FOR TOMORROW AS WELL AS TODAY

Communication must be aimed primarily to meet the needs of a given situation in the present. If it is to be accepted by the receiver it must also be related to the common past — social, cultural and personal. Most important of all, however, it should be consistent with the long-term interests of the future. For certainly we have to live with the consequences of today's communication in our tomorrows, be it for good or ill.

In practical language communicating for tomorrow means the ability to speak to the purpose and aims of an organization, or individual — what they hope to do and be in the future. Of course the situation, the general conjunction of circumstances, will shape the lives of both corporations and individuals, but — as we look ahead — there is a degree of choice before us. Communicating about that choice, and the values which can act as compass bearings guiding us in an as yet unformed future, should complement the mass of daily communications which jump from moment to moment. Awareness of the future, a distinctively human characteristic, makes communication more difficult, but enriches it. Sometimes it takes courage to communicate for tomorrow, but if we can bring ourselves to do so the people of tomorrow will rise up and thank us.

9 BE SURE YOUR ACTIONS SUPPORT YOUR COMMUNICATIONS

Actions speak louder than words. If someone's attitudes or actions contradict his words, our tendency is to discount what he says. Thus, in industry, communication is no substitute for sound management practices on the one hand, and integrity on the other. Action in this context is a wide term, embracing a foreman showing new employees how to do the job at one end of the spectrum, to a chairman or managing director establishing proper systems or procedures for communication at the other end. An action is what you do, as opposed to what you say. Words should interpret what is done, and action should accompany words. The test of our words is whether or not we are willing, if the situation requires, to back them with action.

Thus, if you wish to improve your communication it helps to understand this dynamic relation between word and act. Gifts of oratory or an elegant style are pleasing accessories, but it is action — what you do — which really gets the message across. Make your communication more about the central action; look on your actions more as communications. Eventually our words should become acts, and our acts our truest words.

10 LAST, BUT BY NO MEANS LEAST: SEEK NOT ONLY TO BE UNDERSTOOD BUT TO UNDERSTAND — BE A GOOD LISTENER.

The art of being a good communicant has occupied many pages of this book. In particular Chapter Six on listening, Chapter Eight on reading and Chapter Ten on appraisal interviews included some practical suggestions for improving your abilities as a receiver. Now is a chance to turn back and check those suggestions against your own diagnosis of your 'training needs'. Few of us, for example, are perfect listeners. For not many of us understand how much we can give to others by the simple act of giving them our whole attention. The heart has its reasons, but often we are not attuned to listen to them. For the listener must penetrate to the other's meaning without forcing his way in. He has to listen to what is not spoken — the implicit meanings and the hidden undertones, what is left half-said or unsaid.

One method for improving our powers of understanding is to concentrate on asking questions rather than rushing in with comments. Questions should pleasantly extend a speaker, like searching returns on a tennis court. We can also improve our 'feedback': giving others an accurate idea of whether or not we are clear about their meaning, either verbally or by some non-verbal method such as a smile or a nod. Like justice, listening should not only be done: it should be *seen* to be done.

*　　*　　*

Like all arts, communicating should be a natural and largely unconscious activity. But in learning any art or skill there must be times when we are thinking consciously about it, or about some artificially isolated strand which goes to make up the whole. A textbook can give exercises, and they are as necessary for the beginner in communication as books of piano scales are for the embryo musician. But by the time we have left school or college we have already learnt a great deal about communication. And further progress can best be made by a form of 'action research', i.e. by seeking to change what we do by reflecting *before* and *after* some identifiable piece of communication, if possible with the help of others.

Courses on communication, such as that described in the preceding chapter, can assist by high-lighting the principles and the rules, as well as by providing opportunities for practice and observation. But not all of us will be able to attend them. Moreover progress in any art should lead to the student becoming his own teacher, so that we become our own target-setters and chief critics. Just as self-discipline should replace an imposed discipline, so artistic evaluation becomes more-and-more an internalized function of our better selves. Thus we do not have to be told if we have failed to communicate, or fallen short as listeners or readers: we are instantly aware of the fact. Such travellers may dispense with a guide-book altogether in time, or merely return to it in order to refresh their knowledge of a journey they once made.

As we become our own tutors, like any mature practitioner of an art, it is important not to neglect that other important function of a teacher — encouragement. Most of us have notched up many communication failures in our personal, social and professional life. But we have also known those times when the magic of a true communication happened. Doubtless we contributed only our small part to those experiences, but it is always instructive to analyse the reasons why they went so well. It does not follow that the same approach will work next time, for the other elements in the Communication Star may be different. Yet the process of analysing our successes in the light of the Star model, as well as the principles and rules set out above, will help to educate that inner teacher who alone can guide us to realize our full potential.

Besides its more tangible and mundane benefits — higher performance and salaries, better relationships — we should recall that the rewards of good communication include the endless delights of being understood — and understanding. For all artists are paid in the coinage of joy.

CONCLUSION

The major aim of this book has been to describe and explore the art of communication in such a way that you may feel inspired to set about a practical programme for improving your own communicating. Most of its pages have been devoted to the elements which are present in any communication: the communicator, aim, content, methods, communicant and situation. Awareness and understanding of these elements constitute the first steps towards becoming better at communication.

The art of communication is essentially a practical one. It includes skills such as speaking, listening, writing and reading which we all do, but which few do excellently. These basic skills can all be improved by the conscious effort of applying principles or rules to our daily practice of them. Like learning a new language, this conscious phase may seem awkward and full of mistakes at first. But it is not unnatural, for art lies in perfecting our natural gifts. Eventually these efforts will drift into the depth mind and continue to influence attitudes and actions without us being fully conscious that they are doing so.

A programme for improving one's own communication can be greatly helped by participation in a 'training for communication' course. The reason for this will by now be obvious. The face-to-face communication on a course or conference is a much more potent form than any writing can be. Most of us are stimulated into action by talking and listening ourselves into it — not by reading. It is when our interest is thoroughly aroused and we have set our own sails, that we may turn with most profit to reading to develop and enrich those insights.

One exception to this rule (and I cannot but hope there will be others) is the training manager. As the development of the organization and the individual together feature ever more boldly in the list of training needs, the training manager will have to design courses or programmes which include a succinct study of communication. Chapter Eleven considers the offered objectives and principles for framing a short course embracing the main topics worthy of any busy manager's time and attention.

The training philosophy and methods advocated in Chapter Eleven – practice, observation and participation – are common to the other books in this trilogy – *Training for Leadership* and *Training for Decisions*. Taken together these books now cover the following topics: leadership, motivation, decision-making, problem-solving, creative thinking, the art of communication, the content and methods of communication in organizations, the skills of communication, meetings, interviews and training principles. In all these topics I have tried to select and present the essentials first, bearing in mind the practical concerns of managers or professionals in any organization. Thus, in many places, the bare bones need the extra flesh to be found in further reading as recommended in the 'Notes and References'. But taken as a whole, and centred on the master model of the three overlapping circles as the linking theme, the trilogy does offer some tangible suggestions for an integrated course on 'the human side of enterprise'. To this end all the sessions – the individual bricks that make up the wall – have been thoroughly tested with managers first, sometimes many thousands of times. Much is to be gained if these topics can be seen and presented as a whole.

Throughout my writing of the three books I have been aware that art, skill, craft and technique are only a part – although a vital part – of the answer. As in the cases of leadership and effective thinking, communication reserves its higher peaks of experience and achievement for those people who are touched already by what most of us must strive for with effort. Nor should we envy their ease and natural grace: they are the yardsticks and pace-makers for our own achievement. In them we see the restoration of that lost unity between the two meanings of the word *good,* namely, technical proficiency or skill in a craft on the one hand, and moral goodness and integrity on the other hand.

It is the 'sea of misunderstanding' which isolates us as nations, organizations, groups and individuals into islands, at least according to the words of George Eliot which stood at the head of Chapter One, defining our major problem for us. Gradually, however, through the exercise of good leadership, served by the marvellous intellect of man and his unique potential for communication, those seas of chaos and misunderstanding may yet yield their ground. And eventually we may all come to act and rest as naturally good communicators do already in the sure knowledge that 'No man is an island, entire of itself, every man is a piece of the continent, a part of the main.'

APPENDIX 1

SOME TECHNICAL POINTS
ON THE USE OF THE VOICE

From: *Communication in Industry*, edited by C. Chisholm (London, Business Publications, 1957), pp. 261–4.

When speaking on the more formal occasion, the most comfortable stance is to have your feet placed slightly apart and the weight of the body thrown slightly forward on to the balls of the feet. There is then no fidgeting or unnecessary movement. What gesture, if any, is made springs spontaneously from the words which are on the speaker's lips.

All movement is dangerously expressive of personality. Nervous fidgeting is intolerable. You *must* learn to control it. The constant smoothing of the back of the hair, a rhythmic rising on to the toes, the fastening and unfastening of the inside button of a double-breasted jacket, all these are merely controllable nervous habits.

THE CAUSE OF PLATFORM NERVES

'Platform Nerves' are an almost universal complaint. They are merely the evidence of a nervous system that is functioning adequately. Without it, no speaker is able to see himself in relation to his audience, his subject or the occasion. He is able to see only himself! Hence he cannot project his personality across to an audience, cannot influence people. 'Butterflies in the stomach' are an evidence of that nervous energy essential to successful speaking. There is no cure.

Six physical aids to confidence

1. Breathe well down into your lungs. This enables your diaphragm to control the release of breath from your lungs as you utter each word.

2. If your hands seem to 'get in your way' clasp them loosely in front of you, or place them behind your back. Train yourself to forget them.

3. Look at your audience all the time you are speaking, and embrace them all in your glance. Coyness of glance produces reticence of speech.
4. Let your movements be deliberate and *unhurried*. In a big hall, make them a little larger than life.
5. Do not let your rate of utterance exceed your rate of thought. Only so can you avoid the danger of 'stumbling' over your words.
6. When the occasion is a talk over your desk allow yourself two minutes to clear your mind of the matters which have been occupying it. Compose yourself and relax. Your visitor will do the same.

Here is a set of mental aids.
1. Act as if you are already the possessor of supreme self-confidence.
2. Recall to your mind the picture in outline of your *next* argument or word picture or group of facts while you are dealing with the present one.
3. Try to forget yourself in the urge to communicate − in the enthusiastic desire to deliver your message.
4. Do not think now of *words* − think only of ideas and mind-pictures. The moment will clothe the vivid mind-picture in words.
5. Be yourself. Do not attempt to assume the personality of some character of your imagination labelled 'Orator'.
6. Practise before a critic whenever you can. When you hear his criticism ask yourself 'Why?' Find the answer and rectify the cause of the fault, not merely the symptom.

INFLECTION
'Inflection' is the name given to the tune of our voices − the glides that it makes up and down the scale. Someone has indicated to you some plan of action which he intends to take. You are mildly horrified by it, and say, 'You can't do that!' Will you imagine that situation and speak those words now?

If your imagination has really conjured up the situation in your mind, you will find that your voice has followed a definite tune. Say it again slowly. You will probably find that the words have taken this tune:

You: fairly high up in the scale.
Can't: noticeably lower.

Do: still a little lower.
Tha-at: commencing on the same note as 'do', and then gliding up
        as high as the word *you*.

By that little tune, you have not only expressed your views, but you
are showing how surprised you are that such a plan should have been
suggested.

It is important that you should not think of working out, as it were,
a scale of inflections and adhering to it slavishly. If only you will allow
it, your voice will assume these variations. It is merely a matter of
losing your inhibitions. These dictate to you 'Don't betray your
feelings'. In a public speech you *must* show your feelings if you are to
convince. For simplicity, I have called inflection the 'tune' of your
voice. Just as in music a tune is pitched in a certain key, so are the
inflections of your voice in speech. That key is called the voice's 'pitch'.
Variety in pitch is a further quality of the expressive voice.

There are three pitches, 'high', 'low', and 'normal'. These are relative
terms and depend upon the compass of the speaker's voice. The average
man makes too little use of the impressive lower register of his voice. It
can be cultivated gradually simply by steady consistent use.

Tone quantity and quality
Tone quantity is the loudness or softness of the voice, and tone quality
is its hardness or mildness.

For purposes of expression, the raised voice is quite often hard and
intense, and the lowered, mild.

Line 13 of Antony's funeral oration from *Julius Caesar* — 'He was
my friend, faithful and just to me' — should be spoken in a lowered,
mild almost longing tone. Later, when Antony says, 'O Judgment!
Thou art fled to brutish beasts, And men have lost their reason', you
raise your voice and it becomes hard.

The pause
Most inexperienced speakers are afraid to pause in their speeches. This
may be largely due to the fear that, once they stop speaking, they will
not be able to start again! The effective use of the pause is however
even more difficult than it looks.

Even when you are using notes and you glance down to them after
having made a point, you must be sure before doing so, to keep your
eyes on the audience for a moment. A point loses tremendously in
strength, if the speaker drops his eyes directly he has made it.

You will remember the listener's 'barbed-wire defences'? They have their effect upon the good speaker's pauses too. In effect, he will be 'slow bowling' ideas to his audience, giving them time to play each one with their minds. There must be nothing of the hurricane demon bowler about him! He says, 'Here you are ... Here's an idea ... Got it? ... Good! ... Well, hold tight, because ... here comes another!' *Not*, 'Here's-an-idea-and-another-and-another!' Bowling too many ideas in too short a space of time merely bewilders an audience.

Remember that what seems to you the pause of an age, seems to your audience merely a tiny and acceptable break.

FACIAL EXPRESSION

Has it ever occurred to you how inextricably linked are facial and vocal expression? A speaker with an immobile face invariably has a monotonous voice. A woeful expression can only result in a dejected tone.

Mobility of facial expression (not facial contortion) is necessary to the speaker for three reasons:

(a)   It reflects his attitude, shows his audience how he feels for his subject.
(b)   It affects his voice.
(c)   It is an intrinsic part of the 'communicative behaviour' of the speaker. (Do we not instinctively want to see as well as hear a speaker?)

That facial expression affects the voice is easily proved. Have you ever had to chide a child for some small and really rather ludicrous naughtiness? Your inclination has been to smile while scolding but you have realised that this would bewilder the child. So perhaps you have rubbed your forehead to hide your smile as you spoke. Was the child taken in? Not a bit of it! It is impossible to *sound* angry unless you *look* angry.

A sparkle of enthusiasm on your face induces a similar quality into your voice. A look of gravity induces grave tones. The agonised look on the face of many speakers, finds its way into the anxious sound of their voices. May I repeat myself on this. Coyness of glance produces a reticence of speech.

We have mentioned 'communicative behaviour'. Let me explain it by using the analogy of music. When you sit back merely to enjoy − not technically to analyse − a piece of music, are you consciously aware of the 'pom-pom, pom-pom' of the trombones, the trill of the flute and so on, as separate components of the work? Are you not rather aware of

186

the entire symphonic effect of the *combination* of sounds?

If a speech pleases, grips, interests, informs — the qualities essential to a speech — it is not because you are conscious of the effect of each of its components. It is because the whole attitude of the speaker combines to produce an *overall* effectiveness. Knowledge, design, narrative, all the arts of good delivery, are combined to make up communicative behaviour.

Consider what Fordyce wrote of Demosthenes, 'He that *only hears* Demosthenes, loses much the better part of the oration.'

EMPHASIS

Emphasis is used in speech to give prominence to the 'key' words of a sentence, the more important inferences, and to the conclusions upon which a speaker's arguments are based. It is to a sentence what accent is to a word.

For example, in the word 'Hippodrome', the first syllable 'Hip' is the accented one. In the sentence, 'I saw the play at the Hippodrome', when it is intended merely as a statement of fact, the emphasised words are, 'saw', 'play', and 'Hippodrome'.

Words are emphasised by any or all of the contrasts which we have been considering in this chapter. That is by variations in:

Inflection and pitch.

Phrasing and pace.

Tone, quantity and quality.

Pauses.

Facial expression.

Gesture and movement.

It is for the speaker to decide what form of emphasis he will use remembering that contrast with surrounding words is the criterion.

APPENDIX 2

A CHECK LIST FOR REPORT WRITERS

STRUCTURE AND LAYOUT
(a) Is the title page complete and well laid out?
(b) Is the layout clear and easy to follow?
(c) Are any essential parts of the structure missing?
(d) Are the main parts of the structure in the most suitable order for this report?
(e) Do headings stand out?
(f) Is the numbering of paragraphs uniform?
(g) Are the appendices clear and helpful?

CONTENT
(a) Is the summary or abstract (if included) confined to essentials and a fair statement?
(b) Does the introduction state clearly:

   (i) The subject and the purpose of the report?
  (ii) The date of the investigation?
 (iii) By whom the report was written?
 (iv) For whom the report was written?
  (v) The scope of the report.

(c) Does the main part of the report contain all the necessary facts and no unnecessary information?
(d) Is the order of the main part of the report right?
Is the problem clearly stated?
Does detail obscure the main issue?
(e) Are the sources of facts clear?
(f) Do conclusions follow logically from the facts and their interpretation?
(g) Are possible solutions abandoned without reason?

188

(h)　Are terms used, e.g. abbreviations, symbols, etc., suitable and consistent?

(i)　Are there any statements whose meaning is not quite clear?

(j)　Are facts, figures, and calculations accurate?

GENERAL

(a)　Is the report objective?

(b)　Are there criticisms which can be made of the report's recommendations?

(c)　Is the report efficient and businesslike and likely to create a good impression?

(d)　Could a non-technical man directly or indirectly concerned with the report understand it?

(e)　Could anyone reasonably take offence at anything in the report?

(f)　Is the report positive and constructive?

(g)　Does it make clear what decision, if any, is required and by whom?

(Reproduced with permission from
the National Coal Board's
Report Writing Manual.)

APPENDIX 3

THE ART OF THE LECTURE

In the present climate of opinion or educational methods, however, it is necessary to argue this case. For many teachers and trainers do not believe it, having themselves been on the receiving end of so many boring or irrelevant lectures in their time. In his book *Communication and Learning* (1969), L. S. Powell has some wise words and useful evidence to offer on the importance of good lectures:

> The opponents of lecturing hold that few people are capable of really good lecturing, that the lecture often invites insincerity and showing off on the part of the lecturer and posing on the part of the audience and, perhaps more important, that it does not fulfil a truly educative function since it represses the learner's initiative and reduces his role to that of a recipient of ideas instead of an active participant in their generation.
>
> Many of the pronouncements made on the relative effectiveness of different modes of communication take no account of the widths of the spectra of abilities, subjects and circumstances. No critic would regard the physically passive audience at a symphony concert as ill-served nor would he assess the success of the performance by testing for the retention of certain phrases taken out of context. Some groups of ideas are akin to the coherent sequence in a symphony and can be presented only by sustained and delicately balanced arguments which are more readily comprehensible to some people when they are heard than when they are read. In such circumstances the lecture is an appropriate mode of presentation. Here the lecturer demonstrates how he, the master craftsman as it were, produces his masterpieces. He can show the sequence, draw attention to the pitfalls, highlight that which is of great significance because he knows so well. To chop up such a demonstration (by

discussion technique, for example), however well the joints may be concealed, presents the audience with something different from the whole in the same way as a symphony played in instalments would be different in quality from the whole. At such a lecture the learners are responding to and developing the discipline which lies behind the capacity to be creative.

The Report of the University Grants Committee on methods summarized the evidence in favour of lectures as follows:

Immature university students learn more readily by listening than by reading.

Lectures are especially valuable for introducing and opening up a subject and students can thus be led into subjects which would otherwise prove too daunting for them.

It is easier to co-ordinate lectures (than tutorials etc.) and laboratory work.

Where knowledge is advancing rapidly textbooks may not be available.

Lectures awaken a critical attitude in students.

Lectures can provide aesthetic pleasure.

Inspiring teachers, by lecturing, can infect far more students.

Lectures are economical of staff time.

This report referred to university lectures in 1964 when ten per cent of groups attending lectures numbered less than five students and six *fewer* per cent of groups were over one hundred. In the next year the Robbins Committee stated it saw little value in formal lectures delivered to small audiences.

The American Committee on the Utilization of College Teaching Resources did not support the widely held view that small classes were essential to the most efficient learning. It stated that 'more students are capable of working independently of classroom instruction than have been given the opportunity ... but they require to be prepared for independent study to get the fullest benefit from it.' As part of this preparation for independent study, the Committee included lecturing to very large groups by good lecturers. It strongly recommended that every institution should be organized to provide for groups of a wide variety of sizes including very large ones.

As with kissing, clinical tests can prove that lecturing is a 'bad thing'. Indeed, the comparison can be taken further. Those who have never participated in a good lecture cannot know its power to inspire: its full impact can only be appreciated by consenting adults; its effectiveness is usually dependent in part upon effective visual aids. And, furthermore, despite all the protests, it is going to remain an important mode of communication for a considerable time to come.

The special quality of a successful lecture to a large group is the air of occasion which surrounds it — the size of the lecture hall, the shifting groupings of people, the shuffling hush of conversation which snuffs out as the proceedings begin, the vote of thanks and the applause. This is more than somebody talking to people. The lecture content too is special. It will have been prepared, rehearsed, arranged and, if necessary, spiced with verbal asides or illustrations. A lecture is often the culmination of the work of many people: those who prepare the hall, invite the audience, control the lighting, check the acoustics, introduce the lecturer and cope with the wide range of details which escape notice unless they are overlooked.

The successful lecturer will have learned certain abilities. He will be able to exploit the responses special to crowds — those strange responses of expectancy, humour, inspiration and the like which can be evoked only with large audiences and which have their roots in some incomprehensible form of communication so highly developed in certain kinds of gregarious animals. His response to his audience and his accommodation to his subject are the strategies of the craft, not the rules. The strategies are the lecturer's personal interpretations and although they may be modified by his knowing the rules by which he should lecture they are not determined by them.

The rules of lecturing, on the other hand, the guidelines, are the procedures which are generally followed by successful lecturers. These include ways of structuring a lecture, how to stand and so on. But like the rules for happy marriages they may be broken by the most experienced of practitioners but should never be ignored by the novice.

In a successful lecture a person and a particular area of his competence are presented to a willing audience which is capable of assessing them critically. Matching the lecturer and his subject on the one hand with the audience on the other is essential to success since during a lecture there is no overt feedback from the listeners, and although able lecturers sense rapport, and make adjustments to maximize it as they lecture, they should not be forced to make major modifications to their prepared plan. This throws the initial responsibility for success on the organizer who, in addition to his function as a promoter and manager, must also bring together a lecturer and audience who are compatible one with the other.

The purposes for which lectures are particularly suitable are:

1. to give a general idea of the scope and content of a subject which is to be studied in detail later;
2. to stimulate interest in a subject or line of action or thought;
3. to present a new thesis or technique;
4. to persuade people of their own capacity to understand or enjoy; and
5. to provide an aesthetically stimulating experience and, to quote the greatest of all lecturers, – Michael Faraday: 'A flame should be lighted at the commencement and kept alive with unremitting splendour to the end.' (*Advice to a Lecturer*, Michael Faraday, The Royal Institution.)

NOTES AND REFERENCES

Chapter 1. *The Nature of Communication*
1. Jane van Lawick-Goodall, *In the Shadow of Man*, London, Collins, 1971, last chapter
2. Sir James Gray, *The Listener*, 3 September, 1959.
3. Michael Argyle, *Social Interaction*, London, Methuen; New York, Atherton Press, 1969. See also *Non-Verbal Communication*, ed. R. A. Hinde, Cambridge University Press, 1971.
4. Reuel L. Howe, *Herein is Love*, Chicago, The Judson Press, 1961, p. 102.
5. Published by Management Publications Ltd for the British Institute of Management.
6. William G. Scott, *Human Relations in Management*, Homewood (Illinois), Richard D. Irwin, 1962, pp. 196—203.
7. *Human Communication Theory: Original Essays*, ed. Frank E. X. Dance, New York, Holt Rinehart and Winston, 1967, pp. 295—6.

Chapter 2. *The Communication Star*
1. G. C. Heaviside, 'The Principles of Communication', *Personnel Management*, September 1966.
   A Case History of Poor Communication
   Cecil Woodham-Smith, *The Reason Why*, London, Penguin ed. 1958, pp. 228—37. For a fuller discussion of the 'reason why', see H. Moyse-Bartlett, *Louis Edward Nolan and his influence on British Cavalry*, London, Leo Cooper, 1971, especially Chapter Ten.

Chapter 3. *Organizations: Methods of Communication*
1. *The Times*, 24 March 1971.
2. A. A. Etzioni, *Comparative Analysis of Complex Organizations*,

New York, The Free Press of Glencoe, 1961, p. 137.
3. L. Thayer, *Communication and Communication Systems in Organizations, Management and Interpersonal Relations*, Homewood, Ill., Richard D. Irwin, 1968.
4. *Daily Telegraph*, 30 November 1970.
5. *Communication in Industry*, ed. C. Chisholm, London.
6. Business Publications, 2nd edn, 1957, pp. 22–3.
7. Peter F. Drucker, *The Practice of Management*, London, Heinemann, 1955, pp. 370–1.

Chapter 4. *Organizations: Methods of Communication*
1. D. S. Pugh (*et al*) 'Organisation Structure, Organisational Climate, and Group Structure: an Exploratory Study of their Relationships', *Occupational Psychology*, Vol. 45 No. 1, 1971.
2. *Industrial Society*, July 1971.
3. *The Manager's Responsibility for Communication* (1971), p. 16.
4. See A. Irvine, *Improving Industrial Communication: A Basic Guide for Line Managers*, Industrial Society and Gower Press, 1970, Part Four.
5. *Sunday Times*: 10 October, 1971.
6. This point is well illustrated in Stephen Crane's famous novel of the American Civil War, *The Red Badge of Courage*
7. From R. Aurner and M. P. Wolf, *Effective Communication in Business*, Cincinnati, South-Western Publishing Co. 1967 (5th edn).
Eisenhower Case History.
Dwight D. Eisenhower, *Crusade in Europe*, New York, Doubleday, 1948, pp. 314, 420–2.

Chapter 5. *Effective Speaking*
1. John Casson, 'Are You Getting Through', *Industrial Society*, November, 1970.
2. See *Training for Decision*, Chapter One.
3. Quoted in R. Lewin, *Montgomery as Military Commander*, London, Batsford, 1971, p. 11.
4. *Nelson's Letters*, ed. G. Rawson, London, J. M. Dent, 1960, p. 457.
5. Quoted in *Training for Decisions*, p. 45
6. Bertrand Russell, *Portraits from Memory*, Allen and Unwin, 1956.
7. John Casson, *op. cit.*

8. *The Observer*, 16 August 1970.
9. *Daily Express*, 5 January 1972.
10. *The Practice of Management*, p. 340.

Chapter 6. *Better Listening.*

1. Rosemary Stewart, *Managers and Their Jobs*, London, Pan Books edn, 1970, p. 150.
2. Ralph G. Nichols, 'Listening, What Price Inefficiency?', *Office Executive*, April, 1959. Mr Nichols is Head of the Department of Rhetoric at the University of Minnesota.
3. Ralph G. Nichols, 'How good are you at listening?', *Teamwork in Industry*, April, 1969.
4. Robert T. Oliver, quoted in D. A. Barbara (see below), p. 111.
5. *Op. cit.*, p. 112.

Further Reading

Dominick A. Barbara, *The Art of Listening*, Springfield, Ill., Charles C. Thomas, 1958.
Ralph G. Nichols and Leonard A. Stevens, *Are You Listening?*, New York, McGraw-Hill, 1957.

Chapter 7. *Clear Writing*

1. Rosemary Stewart, *op. cit.*, p. 38
2. Michael Ivens, *The Practice of Industrial Communication*, London, Business Publications, 1963, p. 146.
3. *Fortune*, November 1950.
4. G. H. Vallins, *Better English*: Pan Books, 1953, p. 8. As an example of the kind of textbook available for the young person training for entry into industry or commerce at technical colleges, see P. Little, *Communication in Business*, London, Longman, 1965 (2nd edn. 1970).
5. Sir Ernest Gowers, *The Complete Plain Words*, HMSO, 1954, pp. 91.
6. Philip Oakes interview with Geoffrey Grigson, *The Sunday Times*, 23 January, 1972.
7. Sir Arthur Quiller-Couch, *The Art of Writing*.
8. W. W. Wells, *Communication in Business*, Prentice-Hall, 1968, p. 133.
9. *Timon of Athens*, Act 1, Scene i.
10. Gowers, *op. cit.*, p. 3.
Case History: Lincoln's Letters

Quoted in John D. Glover and Ralph M. Hower, *The Administrator: Cases on Human Relations in Business*, Illinois, Richard D. Irwin, 1957 (3rd edition), p. 256.

Further Reading

For English readers:
H. W. Fowler and F. G. Fowler, *The King's English*, Oxford University Press, 1906 (Third edn, 1931).
H. W. Fowler, *A Dictionary of Modern English Usage*, Oxford University Press, 1926.
Eric Partridge, *Usage and Abusage: A Guide to Good English*, Hamish Hamilton, 1947.
G. H. Vallins, *Good English: How to Write It*, Pan Books, 1951.
G. H. Vallins, *Better English*, Pan Books, 1953. Bound editions of both books by G. H. Vallins were produced by André Deutsch Ltd.
Sir Ernest Gowers, *The Complete Plain Words*, HMSO, 1954.

For American readers:
Rudolph Flesch, *The Art of Plain Talk*, Harper & Row, 1946.
Rudolph Flesch, *The Art of Readable Writing*, Harper & Row, 1949.
Stuart Chase, *Power of Words*, Harcourt, Brace, 1954.
Norman Shidle, *Clear Writing for Easy Reading*, McGraw-Hill, 1951.

For Reference:
The Oxford English Dictionary (in *Concise* or *Shorter* forms) and *Webster's Dictionary* are invaluable to anyone who wants to improve their use of words.
Authors' and Printers' Dictionary: A Guide for Authors, Editors, Printers, Correctors of the Press, Compositors and Typists, compiled by F. H. Collins, Oxford University Press, Tenth edn, 1956. For the spelling of tricky words and personal and place names, for dates of famous men and women, for the meaning and correct form of abbreviations and frequently used foreign words and phrases, for the elucidation of technical terms, and for many other practical purposes in the office and the study, the *Authors' and Printers' Dictionary* is a most helpful guide.
P. M. Roget, *Thesaurus of English Words and Phrases*. Originally published in 1852.

Chapter 8. *The Art of Reading*
1. *Confessions*, Chapter VI, trans. Pusey.
2. G. G. Neill Wright, *Teach Yourself to Study*, London, English Universities Press, 1945, pp. 185—9.
3. In *The Truth About An Author*, cited in Sir John Adams, *The Students Guide*, London, Hodder & Stoughton, 1938, p. 140.
4. There are many textbooks and 'Do-It-Yourself' guides on Rapid Reading available in paperback. Especially recommended: M. and E. DeLeeuw, *Read Better, Read Faster: A New Approach to Efficient Reading*, Penguin, 1965.
5. Francis Bacon, *Essays or Counsels; Civil & Morall*, 'Of Studies' Everyman's Library.
6. G. Birbeck Hill (ed.), *Boswell's Life of Johnson*, London, 1887, Vol. 2, p. 226.
7. *Ibid*, pp. 364—5.
8. E. Bradford, *The Great Siege: Malta 1565*, Penguin Books edn, 1964. For an example of the 'new school' of business histories, see Graham Turner, *The Leyland Papers*, London, Eyre & Spottiswoode, 1972.
9. Published in Pelican Books, 1970.
10. Quoted in A. Jay, *Management and Machiavelli*. See also, A. L. Rowse, *The Use of History*, Hodder & Stoughton, 1946.

Further Reading

H. Bayley. *Quicker Reading*, London, Pitman, 1957.
Kenneth P. Baldridge, *Reading Speed and Strategy for the Business and Professional Man*, New York, Prentice-Hall, 1966.
G. Wainwright, *Towards Efficiency in Reading: Ten Passages for Practice in Faster and More Efficient Reading for Students and Adults*, Cambridge University Press, 1968.
Owen Webster, *Read Well and Remember: A Guide to Efficient Reading*, London, Hutchinson, 1965.

Chapter 9. *Meetings: The Chairman as a Leader*
1. See Chapter Five, 'Sharing Decisions', in *Training for Decisions*, 1971.
2. From Bacon's essay 'On Counsel'.
3. *The Times*, 12 January 1972.
4. Cited in *Training for Leadership*, p. 40.

Chapter 10. *Interviews: Appraising and Being Appraised*
1. Proverbs 9: 7–8 RSV.
2. *Daily Express*, 12 January 1972.
3. George Weinberg, 'How to Make – and Take – Criticism', an article in *Reader's Digest*, (October 1970), condensed from his book *The Action Approach*, 1969.
4. Psalm 141: 5–6 AV.
5. *The Practice of Management*, pp. 342–3.

Further Reading

E. Sidney and M. Brown, *The Skills of Interviewing*, London, Tavistock, 1961.
R. Maier, *The Appraisal Interview*, London, Chapman and Hall, 1958.
'The Appraisal of Appraisals', *Journal of Management Studies*, March, 1964.
Management Appraisal Practices, British Institute of Management Survey, No. 133, March 1967.
Performance Appraisal: What Managers Think, BIM Survey, No. 136, August 1969.
Brian Scott and Barry Edwards, *Appraisal and Appraisal Interviewing*, Industrial Society, Notes for Managers Series, 1972.
M. R. Williams, *Performance Appraisal in Management*, Heinemann, 1972.

Chapter 11. *Courses: Training for Communication*

Further Reading

Case Studies in Human Relations, Productivity and Organization ed. M. Ivens and F. Broadway, London, Business Publications, 1966.
A. S. Irvine, *Improving Industrial Communication*, Industrial Society and Gower Press, 1970.
P. Hesseling, 'Using a Communication Exercise for Training Managers,' *British Journal of Industrial Relations*, March 1965.
P. Hesseling, 'A Communication Exercise for Training Managers', *Personnel Management*, 1965.
M. Deere and A. C. Harns, 'How We Taught Communication', *Technical Education*, August 1966. Description of a course at the Atomic Energy Research Establishment, Harwell.

INDEX